Birding Hot Spots

George H. Harrison

Library of Congress Cataloging in Publication Data

Harrison, George H.
    Roger Tory Peterson's dozen birding hot spots.

    Bibliography: p.
    Includes index.
    1. Birds—United States.   2.   Birdwatching—
United States.   Peterson, Roger Tory, 1908-   I.   Title.
QL682.H37   598.2'073'0973   76-16840
ISBN 0-671-22329-1

Acknowledgments

During the year required to produce this book, I was helped by many, many people. Some were old friends; most were people whom I met for the first time as I worked on the book. Almost all were bird watchers who became caught up in what I was trying to do. Though I am grateful to everyone who contributed in any way to the completion of this work, I want to make special mention of the following:

Roger Tory Peterson, for making bird watching in America what it is today, but specifically for allowing Kit and me to use his list of twelve birding hot spots, and for his personal interest and help in making this book a fact;

My wife, Kit, who was as much a part of this book as I. She accompanied me every inch of the way (except to Tule-Klamath-Malheur), suffering with me from mosquitoes, blackflies, scorching desert heat and sub-zero temperatures on the plains. She shared the joys of success in finding the coppery-tailed trogon, whooping cranes and all the others. She worked at my side through months of editing, retyping and assembling all the material encompassed in these pages. It was a good and very special year for both of us;

My parents, Hal and Mada Harrison, who helped us, encouraged us and actually participated in some of the fieldwork in Arizona while working on a book of their own;

John Strohm, Editor of *National/International Wildlife* magazines, who allowed me all the time needed to do this book while I remained a member of the magazines' staff;

Fred and Mil Truslow, for their encouragement and help, particularly with the Everglades chapter;

Pat and Bud Long, for making us members of their family during our stay on Mount Desert Island, Maine;

The U.S. Fish and Wildlife Service for its complete cooperation during our work on seven National Wildlife Refuges and to these refuge managers and their families for their personal efforts and hospitality: Frank Johnson (Aransas), Wayne Shifflett (Santa Ana), George Unland (Laguna Atascosa), Ned Peabody and Dave Beall (Bear River), Bob Personius and Harold Bushweiler (Horicon) and Bob Fields (Klamath Basin);

Alex Nagy and Barbara Lake, for their interest and help at Hawk Mountain Sanctuary;

Ron Klataske, Tom Logan and Bob Wicht of the National Audubon Society, for their personal assistance at the Platte River;

Brian Morin, for his help while we explored Point Pelee National Park;

William J. Bailey and Bob Connor, for sharing their knowledge of the birding at Cape May;

Lou Rodia and the Cape May County Board of Chosen Freeholders, for help in making life a little easier during Hurricane Eloise;

Howard Lee, for his help in getting photographs of flying geese at Horicon;

Joe and Peggy Hickey, for making possible our day with Roger Tory Peterson at Horicon;

Captain Brownie Brown, for his help in getting us close to 20 whooping cranes on board his boat the *Whooping Crane*;

The following companies for their help: Coleman Camping Equipment, L. L. Bean and Holiday Inn Trav-L-Parks;

And a special word of appreciation to the following experts for reading and commenting on the text prior to final editing: William Robertson (Everglades), Frank Johnson and Wayne Shifflett (southern Texas), Jim Lewis and Ron Klataske (Platte River), Walter and Sally Hoyt Spofford and Jeff and Bunkie Mangum (southeastern Arizona), George M. Stirrett (Point Pelee), Ned Peabody and Dave Beall (Bear River), Bud Long (coast of Maine), Real Bisson (Bonaventure), Alex Nagy (Hawk Mountain), Bob Connor and William J. Bailey (Cape May), Bob Personius (Horicon) and Bob Fields (Tule-Klamath-Malheur);

And finally, the following people, whose photographs are the only ones not taken by me: Ron Klataske, pages 2–3, 71; Alan Brady, page 189; Richard Pough, page 193; Franklin C. Haas, page 192; Rick Solberg, page 67, and Hal H. Harrison, page 14.

*This book is dedicated to
Hal H. Harrison,
my father and my trail guide
through life.*

Contents

Introduction

The cult of bird watching has grown a hundredfold since the turn of the century. In those days the identity of a bird was confirmed over the sights of a fowling piece. The binocular has now replaced the collecting gun, and long lenses are used by those who demand action and are not satisfied by just looking.

We have seen the rise of the "600 Club," those hard-core birders who have seen and identified more than 600 species north of the Mexican border. One of their number, Joseph Taylor of Rochester, has soared well past the 700 mark and is still ascending, searching the far corners of the continent where stragglers from beyond our borders are likely to occur—the Florida Keys for West Indian strays, southeastern Arizona, the lower Rio Grande Valley and the Big Bend of Texas for Mexican goodies, the Aleutians for spillovers from Asia.

I am sure that Joe Taylor—"The Champ"— has been to all of the hot spots described by George Harrison in this book. But I doubt whether anyone, other than George and his bride, has done it in one year. Now that the trail has been blazed, however, I suspect that others will try it.

It must have been at least thirty-five years ago that Hal Harrison, George's father, wrote me that he was leaving his newspaper job in Tarentum, Pennsylvania, to free-lance as a naturalist. My own career, he said, had inspired him to make the move. He rationalized that if a man could free himself to do the things he loved most, why subject himself to the monotony of a 9-to-5 job? Why submit to a subtle form of slavery? Since making that decision, Hal Harrison has distinguished himself as a wildlife photographer, writer and lecturer. He is perhaps best known to the ornithological fraternity for his recently published *Field Guide to Birds' Nests*, the finest treatise on North American birds' nests ever published.

It was during one of the forays of the Brooks Bird Club in West Virginia that Hal introduced me to his son, George, then about twelve, the age when most ornithological obsessives become hooked. I could not have known then that the young man would follow his father's footsteps so closely, first as an editor, then as a free-lance photographer and writer on natural history subjects. When he was Managing Editor of *National Wildlife* and *International Wildlife*, I saw him often; the boy to whom I had pointed out brown thrashers and crested flycatchers was now my editor.

It was no surprise to me when he decided to free himself from editorial responsibilities and do precisely what his father had done—travel, take pictures and write. One of his first major undertakings was this book, the product of an ornithological binge that was to take him to the dozen best bird spots on the continent.

By what criterion does one judge the dozen "greatest"? Number of individuals? Number of species? Rarity? Surely the seabird ledges of the Pribilofs, where a million fulmars, kittiwakes, murres and auklets may be in view at one time, are among the world's greatest bird spectacles, but this archipelago is far out in the Bering Sea, well away from the continent. The masses of Heermann's gulls and elegant terns that breed on Isla Raza are equally spectacular, but that Mexican island too is extralimital.

The gannets of Bonaventure, the cranes of the Platte, the geese of Horicon fall into the category of "spectacular." Cape May Point, Point Pelee, southeastern Arizona and southern Texas offer the greatest variety of species and also the best chances of spotting rarities.

When George Harrison posed the question to me "What are the top dozen?" I was in a dilemma. I could name a hundred places that are fantastic on the right days. And there are days when any one of the top dozen may be disappointing—as at

Hawk Mountain when the wind is from the wrong direction.

After turning over in my mind all of the good birding spots I have known during the past fifty years, I brought things down to the dozen places described in this book. Although other birders may feel strongly about some of their favorite spots and resent the fact that I have omitted them, I stand by my choice. This is my selection.

ROGER TORY PETERSON
Old Lyme, Connecticut

Roger Tory Peterson with the author and the author's sister, Gretchen, at the 1949 Brooks Bird Club Foray, Martinsburg, West Virginia.

George H. Harrison and Roger Tory Peterson birding recently near the Peterson home in Old Lyme, Connecticut.

Foreword

An Idea Became a Birding Year

This book was born on a cold February day several years ago when I visited Roger Tory Peterson at his home in Old Lyme, Connecticut. My visit that day was one of many I had made as Managing Editor of *National Wildlife* and *International Wildlife* magazines, for Roger is a major contributor to both magazines.

During a brainstorming session on story ideas, I asked him, "If you had to make a list of the best places to see birds in North America, where would they be?"

Roger paused for a moment and then said, "There are so many good places."

"Well, let's say the top ten or twelve," I urged.

"That's an interesting idea," he responded.

For the next couple of hours, we listed and relisted Roger's choices of the dozen best places to see birds in North America. The idea never was developed as a *National Wildlife* magazine article, but when Simon and Schuster asked me for some book ideas two years later, this one received the greatest interest from my editor, Julie Houston.

To travel to the twelve best places in North America to see birds would be a lifetime project for some bird watchers. To do it all in a single calendar year was a crazy but challenging plan.

My wife, Kit, and I didn't realize how crazy it really was until we got well into our birding year. Our months of anticipation before leaving for Florida in January were seasoned with great enthusiasm for the project.

The Realities of the Adventure

The experiences we had are documented in the pages that follow, but some of the heartaches, the agonies, the frustrations as well as the satisfactions did not fit into the regular text. Some of it is worth telling here.

First, there are the realities of travel in the mid-'70s. We totaled 32,693 miles getting to and from Roger Tory Peterson's Dozen Birding Hot Spots. We actually drove 25,935 of those miles and flew the other 6,758 on commercial airlines. Nearly all the driven miles were put on our three-year-old Oldsmobile station wagon, which started the year with 57,000 miles on the odometer. We often drove more than 500 miles a day, and on two occasions we topped 900 miles in one stint. This is not intended to be a commercial for GM, but I must say that we had virtually no mechanical trouble with that car. Every time we arrived home in Hubertus, Wisconsin, after a long trip, I breathed a sigh of relief that we had made it . . . *una vez más.*

The cost of gasoline was a major consideration, and nearly every time we needed gas, we shopped. The cost ranged from as high as 81 cents for an imperial gallon in Canada to 43 cents a gallon in Texas.

Then there was the high cost of lodging. Kit and I avoided motels unless forced into them during a snowstorm or hurricane. Most of the time we either tent-camped, using our Coleman equipment, or slept in our station wagon.

Weather influenced every move we made. Without good weather, good photography was not likely, nor were the chances of seeing any birds to photograph. We found our best weather in Florida, Texas and Arizona. Our worst weather began with an approaching blizzard and sub-zero temperatures while we were working on the sandhill cranes in Nebraska in March. In May we endured a late spring snowstorm and 30-mph winds at Bear River Refuge in Utah. In September we rode out Hurricane Eloise at Cape May, New Jersey. But in all places, we waited for good weather and got it.

The camera equipment I used was made by Leica. I have two Leicaflex bodies and four lenses: 35mm, 60mm, 135mm and 400mm. When flash was required, I used portable Honeywell Strobinar electronic units. My black-and-white film was Kodak Plus-X Pan, and my color film was Kodachrome 64.

Timing was very important. We had to be at each hot spot when it was "hot." Fortunately, most of the twelve hot spots heated up at different times. We did, however, have two periods when we wanted to be in two places at the same time. When we finished in Arizona in mid-May, we knew that Point Pelee, Ontario, was the next spot to be hot. However, Bear River, Utah, was also at its best in mid-May. To solve this problem, we drove from Arizona to Salt Lake City, left the station wagon there and flew home. From there we drove our other car to Point Pelee. When we finished in Ontario, we reversed our tracks, and upon arriving back in Salt Lake City we drove to Bear River, in northern Utah. This was all done in a week. The other close call was at Hawk Mountain and Cape May. These two places, however, proved close enough together to enable us to be at both spots during the same week. Our only conflict fell on September 22, the big day at Cape May. We should also have been at Hawk Mountain that day for the biggest flight of the year.

Worth It All

But with all these frustrations, we did have an experience of a lifetime. The people we met, the places we came to know, and the birds we saw made it all worthwhile. We totaled 402 species for the year, including some seen en route to the spots and at home in Wisconsin.

We encourage anyone interested in spectacular birding to visit all twelve of these spots, but we do not recommend doing it in a single year. As I said, it's crazy.

Sport of Bird Watching

One of the fastest-growing sports, indoors or out, is bird watching. It is inexpensive, requires no special education or training and can be enjoyed by almost anyone at any place and time. Bird watching can be enjoyed from a car; through a kitchen window; while you're gardening, golfing, swimming, hunting or fishing, or even while you're on the job as a dentist, a governor, a telephone lineman or a truck driver. I have known people in each of these positions who were dedicated bird watchers.

In fact, about the only requirement for becoming a bird watcher—or "birder," as we often call ourselves—is an interest in seeing birds and learning differences in their individual characteristics.

A pair of binoculars, a bird identification book and old clothes are the only equipment a birder needs to enjoy the sport. Binoculars of 7x35 power are most commonly recommended for the best combination of magnification, light and portability. The most popular bird identification book is Roger Tory Peterson's *A Field Guide to the Birds,* published by Houghton Mifflin. There are other good books, but the Peterson *Field Guide* has been the birder's bible since Roger created the first edition in 1934. Old clothes and a comfortable pair of walking shoes or boots make it easier to go into the brush to see a bird at close range.

It isn't always necessary to go into the woods to see birds. The most popular bird watching today is the backyard variety, where birds are attracted to patios and porches through the use of feeders or special plantings that provide food and cover. (For more information on how to invite wildlife to your backyard, write to the National Wildlife Federation, 1412 Sixteenth Street, N.W., Washington, D.C. 20036.)

Another popular form of birding is the "listing game." For the more adventurous bird watcher, this is a challenging effort to list as many different species as possible in a single day, week, year or lifetime. Dedicated birders enjoy keeping a "life list" in which they record every species they have seen. The champion North American life lister is Dr. Joseph Taylor of New York, who at this writing has seen 720 species in North America. Roger Tory Peterson has a North American life list of 659 species. Some go to any extreme to add a new bird to their list. When the Ross's gull was discovered in Massachusetts in 1974, Dr. Taylor was in Nairobi. He reportedly flew home from there solely to see the Ross's gull and then returned to Africa to complete his visit. To meet the listing challenge, birders like Taylor and Peterson become adept at hearing and identifying bird sounds. They are aware of singing birds even while carrying on a conversation or while involved in some completely unrelated activity.

Two terms that will interest readers of this book are the "Christmas count" and the "big day."

A Christmas count is a *census* of the bird population which is taken sometime during Christmas week. Results from Christmas counts around the country are published in the next issue of *Audubon Field Notes*. The Christmas count is governed by strict rules set down by the National Audubon Society and the U.S. Fish and Wildlife Service. Anyone interested in planning a Christmas count should write to these organizations for pertinent information.

The purpose of the "big day" count is to record as many different species of birds as possible. The big day is generally a twenty-four-hour count that runs from midnight to midnight and is usually done at the peak of spring migration.

There are other forms of bird watching. Some people, like me, enjoy photographing the birds they see; others record their songs, while some hunt their nests. There is also a cadre of bird banders who set up mist nets to catch the birds they seek. Recoveries of banded birds provide needed information about bird movements and habits.

But for most, the challenge of birding is simply to be able to identify birds by their field marks and their songs. I have found that the best way for a beginner to learn is to go afield with an experienced person who will identify the species seen and heard. By comparing what is found in the field with the descriptions in the book, it is fairly easy to learn a hundred or more species by sight and sound in a year. I know this can be accomplished because I have watched a number of people do it, including my wife, Kit.

Once hooked, birders will find themselves engaged in a lifelong activity. Birding has become a happy part of many lives. It is an escape, a wonderful way to relax in the outdoors.

GEORGE H. HARRISON
Hubertus, Wisconsin

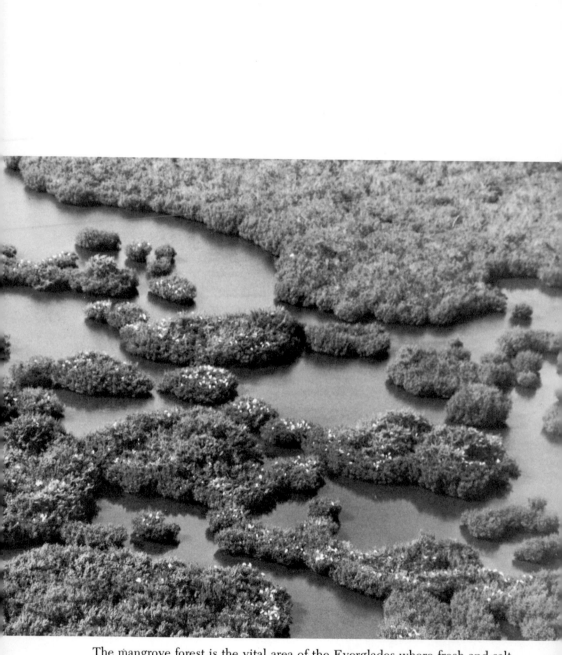

The mangrove forest is the vital area of the Everglades where fresh and salt water meet. Almost every Florida marine species spends part of its life here.

1

Everglades:

A Place for Anhingas and Avocados

In the spring of 1937, when I first visited this sub-tropical wilderness, it was as wild as it was when Ponce de Leon sailed past its southern capes. To all appearances it might have been ten thousand years ago—or a million, for mangroves have looked the same since the Eocene.

—Roger Tory Peterson

Everglades—River of Grass—one of the most intricate biomes in North America, perhaps in the world.

Encompassing nearly all of south Florida, including Lake Okeechobee, the waters of the Everglades move slowly, ever so slowly, 120 miles south to Florida Bay and the sea. Both the east and west coasts of south Florida are slightly elevated, thus forming the Everglades trough through which the broad, shallow river flows. Lying on a submerged plateau, the Everglades is so flat that a difference in elevation of only a few feet can mean a remarkable change in animal and plant life. An altitude of 10 feet is considered "high" in southern Florida.

Our first impression of the Everglades was vastness. Vast stretches of water, land and sky. As far as we could see, there

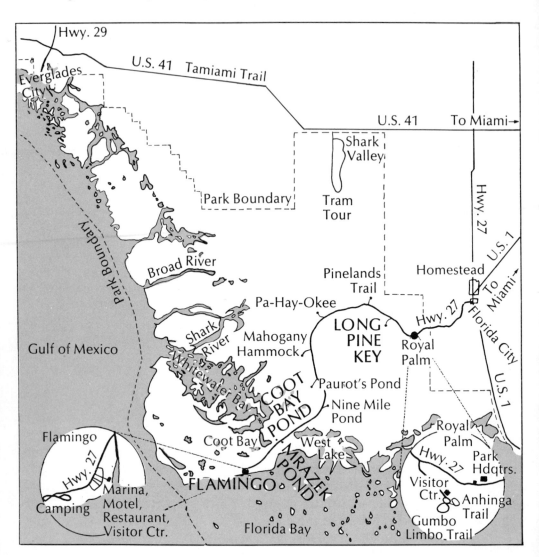

was nothing but saw grass, mangroves, hammocks and slash pine forests.

Americans first became interested in preserving this natural wonder about 1900. In 1915, the Florida Federation of Women's Clubs obtained 960 acres in order to keep intact a particular hammock of royal palms. The state added 4,000 acres in 1921 and called it Royal Palm State Park (present site of Anhinga and Gumbo Limbo trails). The idea of establishing a national park to preserve the Everglades' unique plant and animal life began to catch on during the Depression, but did not become a reality until nearly twenty years later.

Though the park is about twice the size of Rhode Island (1,400,523 acres), it isn't nearly large enough. A quick look at a map of Florida will show you why: the park is only the southernmost 20 percent of the 7,000,000 acres the Everglades encompasses. Much of the rest of the river of grass remains in private ownership, with the State of Florida holding only flowage easements. So fragile is this ecosystem that injury to any part of it has proved to be cancerous to the whole system. There are already 500 miles of major canals through the Everglades, most of which were dug since 1947.

When Harry Truman dedicated America's third-largest national park in 1947 "for all mankind," he had no idea that developments outside the park would continue to destroy its vital fresh water.

The birdlife found in Florida today, though spectacular, is but a remnant of what was there before 1900. William Bartram, traveling there in 1774, wrote that sleep was almost impossible because of "the continual noises and restlessness of the sea fowl . . . all promiscuously lodging together, and in such incredible numbers that the trees were entirely covered." In 1832, Audubon wrote about Sandy Key, "The flocks of birds covered the shelly beaches and those hovering overhead so astonished us that we could for a while scarcely believe our eyes."

A recent example of how man has been killing the Everglades is evident at Coot Bay. As far back as anyone knows, tens of thousands of coots wintered on Coot Bay. During January, coots literally filled this nearly freshwater lake, feeding on the lush aquatic vegetation that grew there. As late as 1952, when my father, Hal H. Harrison, was producing a film on the Everglades, the coots were there in great profusion. Today, there are no coots in Coot Bay. Boating interests prevailed upon the Park Service to construct a canal that would allow boats to enter Coot Bay from Florida Bay. The construction of Buttonwood Canal in

After a swim in Taylor Slough, this anhinga dried its wings at the edge of Anhinga Trail.

the late '50s allowed salt water to flow into Coot and eastern Whitewater bays, killing the aquatic plants the coots fed upon.

But in spite of the many man-made and natural disasters, the Everglades is still one of the great birding spots of North America. Even today few places on this continent can offer a greater variety of beautiful, rare and interesting birds. Most of the species of America's wading birds, shorebirds and water-fowl are still found in the Everglades at some time during the year. Fourteen wildlife species found in the park are listed as "threatened" by the U.S. Fish and Wildlife Service.

So, with a feeling of optimism, Kit and I arrived at the park

Anhingas dried off in the warm Florida sun along the trail named for them.

This battery of photographers were all focusing on a purple gallinule along Anhinga Trail.

entrance on Route 27, 12 miles southwest of Homestead, on January 8. Using a map issued at the gate, we headed immediately for Anhinga Trail, touted as the best place in the park to see birds. After only 2 miles of driving, we pulled into Royal Palm Interpretive Station, gateway to Anhinga and Gumbo Limbo trails.

Though I had heard of Anhinga Trail for thirty years, I found it hard to believe we were there when we drove into the parking lot. All we could see was a building, several quick-lunch and beverage machines, rest rooms and people. Could this be the same Anhinga Trail that had produced all those famous bird and alligator photographs?

Indeed it was. From the parking lot we walked around the building and there was Taylor Slough. Immediately we saw anhingas, alligators, great blue herons, green herons and coots. A little pied-billed grebe sputtered around the slough, a long-toed purple gallinule stepped daintily across the lily pads and snowy egrets wearing golden slippers fluffed their plumes. All this, and we were hardly on the trail! Here certainly was a wildlife photographer's paradise.

A 5-foot alligator slipped into the water on the far bank and approached a small group of nervous coots and gallinules. The birds quickly moved out of its way. Then the gator submerged to the bottom among the gars and bowfins.

Opposite: A great (common) egret fished along Taylor Slough.

Below: All the other wildlife along Taylor Slough gave the resident alligators a wide berth.

Above left: Oblivious of people, a little blue heron fed only a few feet away from Anhinga Trail.

Above right: A sharp-eyed green heron took aim at a passing fish in Taylor Slough.

Below: Blending into the grasses along Taylor Slough, a great blue heron watched the people watching him from Anhinga Trail.

A little blue heron scanned the shoreline with its beady eyes in search of finny morsels. Its head turned first this way, then that, until eye met prey. Then, zap!

A green heron froze in a strained position for endless minutes as it studied the clear water. Without warning, it struck, and a surprised minnow became sustenance.

A great blue heron prepared to fish, but a great egret had a different plan. An apparent rivalry continued as the squawking white bird chased the great blue out of the coveted fishing spot that it regarded as exclusively its own.

Moving along the trail, we spotted a light-colored hawk on a stump in the saw grass. For a moment we were puzzled. What species was it? Yes! Florida's own raptor—a short-tailed hawk. A new one for my life list.

One of the Everglades' most fascinating birds is the one for which the trail is named—the anhinga, snakebird or water turkey, a bird equally at home underwater, on water, on land, in trees or high in the sky. We watched an anhinga drop from her perch into the water and become snakelike searching for small fish. The name "snakebird" comes from its unbirdlike appearance when only its long neck remains above the water. Much of the time the bird was totally submerged and we saw only its dark shape underwater, searching among the weeds for minnows. When a victim was found, the anhinga caught it like a spear fisherman, neatly impaling the prey on its spear-shaped bill. The bird then raised its head and neck, threw the fish into the air and swallowed it in one easy flip. When satiated, the anhinga pulled its wet bulk onto a rock, spread its 47 inches of wet wings and began to dry out in the warm sun.

All these experiences occurred in less than 200 yards of walking.

When we came to the boardwalk, a platform over the ponds of Taylor Slough, our adventures continued. Now the mangroves, willows, pond apples and myrtles closed in on us. A red-bellied woodpecker peered over its shoulder as we walked only 3 feet from it. Crested flycatchers, palm warblers, mockingbirds and more green herons were close enough for short-lens photography.

In a few more yards we were back in the open. A large pond

A quarter of a mile of Anhinga Trail is elevated over Taylor Slough. A myriad of water birds, turtles and alligators can be seen from the boardwalk.

American coots are common in Taylor Slough. This one was feeding on the aquatic vegetation under the Anhinga Trail boardwalk.

surrounded by dense vegetation beckoned us on. Here a small shelter-type interpretive center identified the many birds we saw over the railing.

Coots selected pieces of lacy vegetation, while a Florida terrapin ate the same plants from beneath the surface. An alligator lumbered onto a grassy deck, while another slid off in search of a meal.

All of Anhinga Trail teemed with life—natural life, unmolested, unconcerned.

We visited Anhinga Trail many times during our week in Everglades National Park and were never disappointed. We discovered that the best time to be there was early morning. On January 10, for example, when we arrived at 7:30 A.M., we were practically alone. By 9 A.M., we were joined by only a half dozen other bird watchers, which still gave us the feeling of having the place to ourselves.

On another one of those early January mornings, we met Erwin Winte, the sixty-three-year-old father of Anhinga Trail. Winte, now retired, told us that when the park was established in 1947, he and a few others recommended that this location along Taylor Slough be given special attention for the benefit of park visitors. Despite the lack of funds, Winte and a small corps of dedicated workers built a platform and an earthen-fill parking area along Ingraham Highway, which at that time crossed the slough. For ten years, this 300-foot stretch was all there was of Anhinga Trail. In the late 1950s, it was expanded to its present length of a half mile, including a quarter mile of boardwalk.

There are other places about which park founders may be proud. Though none of them compare to Anhinga Trail for variety of birdlife, visitors should definitely include a visit to Mrazek Pond, 6 miles northeast of Flamingo (32 miles from the park entrance). The days we visited Mrazek we found a large flock of blue-winged teal, coots, great and snowy egrets and tricolored (Louisiana), little blue and great blue herons.

Shortly after arriving at Mrazek Pond late in the afternoon of January 9, we were invited to join a young couple from Pennsylvania who were sitting on a blanket eating snacks as they watched the "show." The blue-winged teal were the main attraction. To feed, the ducks tipped their bottoms up while tread-

Above left: A pair of blue-winged teal fed in Mrazek Pond.

Above right: A tricolored (Louisiana) heron stalked a fish while a blue-winged teal "bottomed up" on Mrazek Pond.

ing their webbed feet in a paddle-wheel motion. Some of them splashed water 2 feet in the air. At times there were more bottoms up than down.

In the midst of the teal show, two great egrets arrived on the scene to wade in the shallow lake. The late-afternoon light made the whole pond a tableau of fine art, and the two big white birds highlighted this colorful scene.

Almost across the road from Mrazek Pond, but a little closer to Flamingo, is Coot Bay Pond. Though it is also famous for roadside bird spectacles, all we found was an active bald eagle nest on the far shore. Through binoculars we could see both birds perched next to their huge platform of sticks.

We were told that it was one of 55 active bald eagle nests in the park. Most of them were located on the tiny keys that dot Florida Bay. Park regulations protect the breeding wildlife on these little islands by prohibiting human intrusion on all but a few.

Route 27 ends at Flamingo on Florida Bay, 38 miles from the park entrance. Don't be deceived as we were by the lodge, cottages, marina, gift shop, museum and ranger-station complex. Flamingo is a gold mine for bird watchers.

An immature brown pelican at Flamingo was a picture of contentment.

We found that the best place to see birds in Flamingo was on the campground located at the very end of the road. Between 7:30 and 8 on the morning of January 12, we saw 56 roseate spoonbills fly directly over us in flocks of 3s and 5s as they headed toward the bay to feed. Imagine bright pink birds with spoon-shaped bills against a deep blue sky! This one experience was worth the trip to Florida for us. It was good to see evidence that the spoonbill population, nearly extinct forty years ago, is safe again.

The campground at Flamingo was virtually alive with birds that morning. A flock of 500 red-winged blackbirds, all males, moved nervously through the tenting area. Picture all 500 taking flight and then banking in unison, showing identical red chevrons on black fields!

A great white heron stood on the beach like a sentinel, as if directing the traffic of dowitchers, semipalmated plovers, semipalmated sandpipers, black-bellied plovers, dunlins and western sandpipers. Though research has proved that the great white heron is a color phase of the great blue, we felt as if we were seeing a new bird.

Still more birds populated the campground that morning.

Laughing gulls, in winter plumage, followed the tour boat at Flamingo.

Tricolored (Louisiana) herons and snowy egrets flew in flocks of nearly 100 in search of quiet feeding pools; the ever-present turkey vultures dipped and soared in the buffeting winds of Flamingo; ring-billed gulls and brown pelicans traded back and forth.

A concession at Flamingo offers a two-hour boat trip into Coot Bay and Whitewater Bay. We took the ride, but do not recommend it for birding. The coots are gone, and the few herons and egrets seen as the boat moves along the canals are not worth the boat fee. The highlight of the boat trip for me was the speech the pilot gave about how man was destroying the Everglades. It was well done.

A word about flamingos. There are flamingos in the park, but not at Flamingo. A wandering band of 13 birds was sighted from the air by park rangers in Florida Bay while we were there. Some speculate that these predominantly white flamingos are color rejects from the Hialeah Race Track flock, but they are more likely young birds.

Another big bird, the Everglades kite, is one of those species that have become well known through attempts to save it from extinction. This snail-eating kite has been seen along the Tamiami Trail (Route 41) and Alligator Alley (Route 84). As we drove across both highways, we kept a lookout for the famous birds. We checked out every vulture and hawk we saw for kite identification markings—white spot on tail, floppy flight, etc.—but we did not see a bird we could definitely call an Everglades kite.

We did see many of the common Everglades birds on both of these major highways and recommend them for birding.

Early on several mornings we noticed a great congregation of egrets, herons, ibis and ducks, all feeding in a frenzy in a roadside canal or park pond. This is what some birders call a "road show." Photography was remarkably easy here, because the birds were so engrossed in their first feeding of the day that they paid little attention to ogling humans.

There are also two more park facilities along Tamiami Trail. At Shark River Valley, the Park Service operates a one-hour tram trip around a loop trail from which typical Everglades habitat and birdlife can be observed. We recommend it, if you have time.

In the northwest corner of the park, at Everglades City, the Park Service operates a marina. Boat trips into the Glades are scheduled hourly from the wharf. One of the most interesting sights we found there was the large flock of black skimmers

Lined up like a platoon of soldiers, black skimmers faced into the wind on the wharf at Everglades City.

parked right on the wharf. The entire flock lifted in a mass as boats moved into and out of the marina. I am always amazed when I watch a large flock of birds maneuver in perfect synchronization.

If you happen to be campers, as we are, check the mosquito situation at Flamingo before camping there. Though the birding is excellent, it was too windy and had too many mosquitoes for us. We preferred Long Pine Key. It was quiet, private and woodsy. We spent very little time in camp, but whenever we were there we enjoyed the songbirds. Mockingbirds, cardinals, towhees, pine and palm warblers, blue-gray gnatcatchers and blackbirds flitted around our tent and table. At night we were serenaded by three barred owls, each trying to outhoot the others. One night, a great horned owl awakened us from sound sleep. What a nice way to be awakened!

The campground rest rooms were well populated at night with bright green tree frogs. Hundreds of them, attracted by the combination of light and water, sat motionless on the walls, in the sinks and around the lights. They were attentive companions as we washed before going to bed each night.

An interesting place to picnic is Nine Mile Pond, 11.5 miles northeast of Flamingo (26.5 miles from the park entrance). The few picnic tables there were rarely filled during weekdays, and the birding was excellent. The resident flock of crows was good enough reason to stop. Entertaining us for at least an hour, they were the tamest 7 crows we've ever seen. First they searched for grubs in the grass around our table, accepting a handout when offered; then, as if in appreciation, they performed aerial acrobatics of a quality found among golden eagles. The 20-to-30-mph breeze enhanced their performance.

A bald eagle, two white-crowned pigeons, pied-billed grebes, royal terns and a number of common songbirds were foils to the "Heckle and Jeckle" bag of tricks.

Birders who go to the Everglades in January get a bonus in the locally grown fresh fruits and vegetables. Homestead is a great truck-farming area. We thought we had suddenly disappeared into August when we found avocados, corn on the cob, tomatoes, squash and green peppers for sale along the roadside. Strawberries were plentiful, too.

Add the fresh vegetables to a bountiful citrus crop, all available at reasonable prices and served up at 70-degree temperatures with lots of sunshine, and you have quite a treat.

No doubt about it, January is the best time of the year to be in Everglades National Park. By then the Christmas rush is over, the camping and picnicking areas are half empty and the wintering birds are most abundant. In fact, January is a great time to be in southern Florida even if you are not a bird watcher.

VISITOR TIPS

Recommended time to visit: January.

Clothing: The average temperature in southern Florida during January is 70 degrees, so summer clothing is in order for the day. For evenings it's a good idea to have long pants and warm sweaters. Although cold spells are rare in this area, it would be wise to be prepared by having along a jacket. Hiking boots are not necessary, since all areas open to the public have excellent paths.

Lodging: There is a motel at Flamingo operated by a park concessioner. There are also many fine motels, running from luxury to economy, in Homestead, Florida City, Everglades City, Ochopee and Chokoloskee. There are none at Shark Valley. You probably won't have any problem finding accommodations after you have arrived, but it would be a good idea to have advance reservations.

Restaurants: In the park you can find vending machines offering snacks and beverages at Everglades City and at Royal Palm, where Anhinga and Gumbo Limbo trails begin. There is a restaurant at Flamingo. Shark Valley, Homestead, Florida City, Everglades City and Chokoloskee also have restaurants.

Camping: There are excellent camping facilities at Long Pine Key for tents and recreational vehicles. Flamingo has a campground for tents and RVs as well as a walk-in camping area for tents only. Private campgrounds can be found in Everglades City and Chokoloskee and along Tamiami Trail between Miami and Everglades City. There are also a couple in the Homestead/Florida City area. Advance reservations may be made at any of the campgrounds, including those in the park.

Picnic Areas: There are beautiful picnicking areas throughout the park. Our favorites were Nine Mile Pond and Long Pine Key, but there are also lovely spots at Flamingo, Paurotis Pond and Everglades City.

Reservations: Reservations should probably be made sixty days in advance—more if they are going to be for Christmas week. The park headquarters (address below) will take reservations for campgrounds in the park from December 1 through April 30 and can also provide names and locations of motels in the area. Write ahead for motel and camping information to:

>Everglades National Park
>Box 279
>Homestead, Florida 33030

>Homestead Chamber of Commerce
>Homestead, Florida 33030

Rest Rooms: Rest room facilities are provided at the Parachute Key Visitor Center (park headquarters), Royal Palm, Long Pine Key campground and picnic area, Everglades City and Shark Valley.

Telephone: The only telephones in the park are at the Parachute Key Visitor Center as you enter the park and at the marina and campground in Flamingo.

Gasoline: In the park you can fill up at the Flamingo marina. Outside the park there are plenty of gas stations in the Homestead/Florida City vicinity, along the Tamiami Trail, in Everglades City and near Shark Valley.

Groceries: If you need supplies and don't want to leave the park, the marina at Flamingo has a small general store. Otherwise, there are grocery stores in Homestead and on the road between Florida City and the park. Most of these places, including the marina, sell ice.

Hospital: The nearest hospital to Everglades National Park headquarters is in Homestead.

Airport: For commercial flights, the closest airport is in Miami. However, Homestead does have an airport that can handle small private aircraft.

Bird List: A checklist of 310 birds of Everglades National Park may be obtained at the Parachute Key Visitor Center.

2

Southern Texas:

Down Mexico Way

In this unique area where, zoologically, East meets West and Mexico spills across the border, it is possible to see more birds in a day than in any other section of the United States. During the flood tide of spring migration it is the mecca of hard-core birders from every corner of the land.

—Roger Tory Peterson

ARANSAS

The sign read, "Aransas National Wildlife Refuge—1 mile." Around the next turn, we were met by three sandhill cranes standing at the edge of the road. As if sent by Refuge Manager Frank Johnson to welcome us, the three huge birds, with necks extended, trumpeted a greeting as our car came to a sudden stop.

We had arrived at the world-famous winter home of the sandhill's rare cousins, the whoopers. Our reception party was an appropriate coincidence.

The 54,000-acre refuge is located on San Antonio Bay just north of Rockport, Texas. It is a mixture of salt marshes and freshwater ponds surrounded by live oak, greenbrier and red bay thickets. This ideal habitat attracts thousands and thou-

sands of wintering waterfowl, songbirds and the wild flock of whooping cranes.

An 18-mile loop road constructed by the U.S. Fish and Wildlife Service permits motorized bird watchers to traverse several interesting habitats and to see as many as 50 species of birds on a single round trip. This one-way paved road crosses numerous freshwater ponds populated with coots and ducks, dense thickets filled with songbirds and open grasslands frequented by white-tailed deer and wild turkeys. Indeed, this

One of the world's rarest birds, a whooping crane, fed along the Inland Waterway at Aransas National Wildlife Refuge.

loop road is so good for birding that it makes Aransas a significant ornithological attraction even without whooping cranes. On our first trip on January 16, we listed such notable species as roseate spoonbills, orange-crowned warblers, white-eyed vireos, white pelicans and snow geese. The sight of wild turkeys herding ahead of our car like cattle was a revelation. We counted 26 turkeys in two flocks.

If you have ever wondered where your favorite robin spends its winters, chances are the answer is Aransas. We saw thousands of robins every day.

In addition to our finding all the other birds, there was always the hope of seeing a whooping crane. Six miles into the loop road we came to an ultramodern observation tower over-looking an excellent whooper feeding ground. This is the only place inside Aransas where the public can see whoopers (if they are lucky). Three high-powered telescopes at the top of the tower helped us identify all whooperlike white birds in the marsh below. We saw great and snowy egrets, white pelicans and snow geese, all white and all large (some even had black wing tips), but no cranes. A push-button taped lecture next to the telescopes described the identification marks of each species of big white birds. It spoke, too, of a family of 3 whoop-ers that fed regularly on the tidal flat below.

From the tower we also saw roseate spoonbills, numerous "peeps," willets, dowitchers, yellowlegs, reddish egrets, common terns and the blue phase of the snow goose (blue goose).

Kit searched for whoopers from the Aransas National Wildlife Refuge tower.

Two pairs of whooping cranes as seen from the *Whooping Crane*.

White-tailed deer and wild turkeys displayed little fear of passing cars.

Farther along the road we found small herds of grazing white-tailed deer. We were surprised at their tameness. By using the car as a blind, and the telephoto lens for close-ups, I was able to make quite a few interesting photographs. We were intrigued by the bucks' antlers. By mid-January, most northern whitetails have shed their antlers, but not these. We also saw other mammals along the loop road, including wild boars, skunks, raccoons, nutria and fox squirrels.

Incidentally, we recommend *not* feeding the fox squirrels at the refuge picnic grounds. These brazen little characters have absolutely no fear of people and will, in fact, threaten you in order to get a handout. People who do feed them are ultimately responsible for their deaths. When they become a nuisance, they have to be destroyed.

At a number of places along the loop road there are parking lots where well-marked and well-maintained foot trails begin.

Most trails are labeled as bird walks, which indeed they are. The one marked "Big Tree" not only led us to four-hundred-year-old live oaks, but was also one of the best birding trails we found in Aransas. On the misty morning of January 17, we walked Big Tree Trail and listed orange-crowned warblers, white-throated sparrows, white-eyed vireos, kinglets, turkeys and thousands of robins and cardinals. The robins rose in waves in front of us. At the pond near the big trees we rested on benches as we watched gadwalls, northern shovelers, pied-billed grebes, American coots and one alligator feeding.

One advantage to getting onto these trails early in the morning is the opportunity to see tracks made in the sand the night before . . . by deer, wild boar and coyotes, among other species.

After several trips around the loop without seeing whoopers, we decided to try the only guaranteed way to see them on their wintering grounds: from the deck of the boat *Whooping Crane*, which sails four days a week from Copano Bay, 9 miles north of Rockport. Piloted by a colorful skipper named Captain

Whooping crane watchers fed the gulls en route to the crane feeding grounds.

Brownie Brown, the *Whooping Crane* leaves the Sea Gun Resort Hotel dock at 1:30 sharp every Wednesday, Friday, Saturday and Sunday from October 20 to April 10.

"We guarantee you will see whooping cranes or your money will be refunded," announced Brownie as we pulled away from the dock.

I asked Brownie how many times he has had to refund the money. "In eleven years," said Brownie, "I have had to refund money only four times. That was because of heavy fog which came in after we were under way."

This was not going to be a refund day. He assured us that we would see and photograph about half of the whoopers known to exist in the wild.

On our way out of the harbor we encountered a little drama. I noticed a laughing gull flying by with a piece of fishing line hanging from its leg. A few minutes later, Brownie announced that a gull was hanging on a piling just ahead of us and that we would take a few minutes to rescue it.

As Brownie edged the *Whooping Crane* in to the piling, the first mate and I plucked the hanging gull off the piling with a pole. The first mate held the bird while I removed the fishhook from its left leg. I felt like a hero as I set Jonathan Livingston free.

The whoopers' feeding grounds are situated along the Intracoastal Waterway. Each whooping crane family occupies a rather large area or territory during its stay at Aransas and defends it from intrusions by other whoopers. The birds feed on blue crabs, marine worms, clams and other marine creatures.

Brownie's tour was 32 miles along the shipping lanes of the waterway. It lasted four hours. Although it was more than an hour before the boat reached whooper habitat, Brownie started talking about and identifying other water birds from the moment we left the dock.

"Let's see how close we can get to this little Forster's tern," Brownie suggested on the P.A. system.

"That big bird with a long neck is a great blue heron," he reported.

"We have a special porpoise mating call on this boat which is 'gar-en-teed' to call in porpoises." And sure enough, the porpoises (bottle-nosed dolphins) appeared right on cue.

Right on cue, the bottle-nosed dolphins (porpoises) surfaced alongside the *Whooping Crane*.

Before long, Brownie had pointed out 60 birds, many of which cannot be seen from the refuge loop road. The new birds for us included the caracara, the white-tailed hawk and the long-billed curlew, bringing our Aransas list to 81 for two and a half days.

As we neared the refuge boundaries, Brownie spotted the first pair of whoopers feeding in the salt marsh about a mile away. He directed all eyes to the two white spots, but he did not slow the boat. He knew that he could get closer to other whoopers just ahead. Then we saw 2 more, and then 3 more, including a brown-headed youngster. All were spotted as our boat continued to move at full speed. Finally, we neared a pair feeding in the shallows, not far from the shipping lane. Brownie slowed the engines and edged the boat in to the shore until we were aground in the mud. One more rev of the engines anchored us securely as passengers with cameras, lenses, binoculars and spotting scopes clattered and shuffled on the deck for a better view.

With the boat securely fastened to the bottom, it became a steady platform for photography. Our captain repeated this procedure several times that day. We got within 100 yards of a feeding pair. Brownie told us that he gets as close as 100 feet when he is lucky.

"I'll collect an extra dollar for that one, folks," Brownie commented as everyone laughed. We would gladly have paid it, too, if he had been serious. What a sight! The world's rarest cranes, right in front of us! He showed us 20 whoopers that day—nearly half of all the wild birds in existence.

Brownie's boat is one of only two commercial boats that take people to see the cranes. However, private boats do explore the edges of the whooper habitat, and this is how some disturbances occur. For that reason, both the Fish and Wildlife Service and the National Audubon Society have wardens and biologists in the area while the whoopers are in residence.

This residence period runs from October 15 to April 15, and visitors can usually see cranes on any day during that time. But according to Brownie, the best time to see and photograph the whoopers is in late February when the birds congregate and dance as their spring courting begins. They also exercise more at that time in preparation for their long flight north.

The story of the whooping crane has been described at times as a "love affair between a great white bird and two nations who have traditionally cheered the underdog." Before the middle of the last century, the range of the whooping crane was from the Arctic coast to central Mexico, and from Utah to South Carolina. Apparently, these birds have never been numerous during recent times, but we do know that before man's interference these relics from the Pleistocene era maintained a stable population.

By the late 1920s, fewer than 50 birds remained to find their way to remote wintering grounds. In 1941, the number was down to 15 in Texas, while only 6 remained in Louisiana. The last of the Louisiana flock of whooping cranes was reported in 1948, and only 30 birds remained in Texas on the Aransas Refuge.

The long migration flight made twice a year exposes the whoopers to their greatest dangers. Leaving Aransas as the weather warms in early April, the birds journey 2,500 miles northward to Wood Buffalo National Park in the Northwest Territories, where they build their nests, hatch their young and rear them to near adult size before returning to Texas. Though the normal clutch is two eggs, usually only one youngster survives.

Some years as few as one or 2 youngsters will arrive in Texas with the adults, though many more may have been hatched. Disease, predators and the long flight south, fraught with many perils, cause annual mortalities to this fragile species.

At the writing of this book, there are about 50 wild whoopers (including several raised by sandhill crane parents in Idaho) and about the same number in captivity.

Though there will always be the risk of natural losses, there have been some new and disturbing man-made threats to the vulnerable birds. The recent construction of oil rigs within sight of the wintering cranes, just off the Aransas shoreline, greatly increases the possibility of annihilation from an oil spill.

There is also the threat of whooping cranes' being shot as they pass through states that permit the hunting of sandhill cranes during fall migration.

Finally, there is the pressure being exerted upon the birds by well-meaning people who want to see them up close at Aransas. Kit and I watched several families of whoopers being flushed by curious people in small boats along the Intracoastal Waterway.

Although the number of whooping cranes has slowly climbed back from the brink of extinction in recent years, their future is still very much in doubt.

SANTA ANA

Our station wagon nosed up sharply as we drove over the top of a Rio Grande levee and down the other side into the Santa Ana National Wildlife Refuge. We were still in the United States, but as far as the trees, birds, mammals and climate were concerned, we were in Mexico. Only a curve in the political boundary put this typically Mexican landscape in our country.

This small remnant of subtropical forest located 45 miles west of Brownsville, Texas, is often referred to as the "gem of the National Wildlife Refuge system." Because of its strategic location along the Rio Grande, this tiny 2,000-acre refuge is famous for harboring many birds usually seen only south of the

Santa Ana National Wildlife Refuge is located on a strategic bend in the Rio Grande River. On the right bank is Mexico.

Loud and relatively fearless chachalacas roam Santa Ana's 2,000 acres like gangs of barnyard chickens.

Strange chickenlike birds from Mexico called chachalacas fed on the birdseed we put out at Santa Ana.

border. Many Mexican species reach their northern limits at Santa Ana.

Our passage on January 19 from the heavily farmed lower Rio Grande Valley into the virgin river-bottom thickets at Santa Ana was delineated by the high levee we crossed at the refuge gate. Before we had gone 100 yards inside the refuge, a small flock of chachalacas ambled across the gravel road in front of us. So tame and so unconcerned were they that we had to stop the car to avoid hitting the chickenlike birds. Their call was bizarre, and when they squawked, the whole thicket vibrated.

Mid-January is an excellent time to visit Santa Ana. Not only is the wintering bird population at its peak, but birds can

A brazen long-billed thrasher fed only a few feet in front of the photo blind.

be seen more easily in January before the trees sprout new leaves.

Most of the birding can be done along the Santa Ana Loop, which is a 6.7-mile one-way gravel road that tours all features of the refuge. The road also passes each of the fifteen walking trails, the longest of which is 1.8 miles. We found that a combination of driving the loop and walking the trails gave us a complete feel of Santa Ana.

One of the memorable sightings along the Santa Ana Loop was a pair of Harris' hawks perched in a high tree near the old Spanish cemetery. We also saw black-crested titmice, long-billed thrashers and great-tailed (boat-tailed) grackles there.

The loop road ends with a quarter-mile drive on the same levee we crossed to enter the refuge. On one of our nights at Santa Ana, Refuge Manager Wayne Shifflett suggested we drive the levee road to see pauraques—Mexican relatives of our whip-poor-will. As our headlights reached into the darkness ahead, we picked up the red reflections of pauraques' eyes on the gravel road ahead of us. When our car neared the red spots, the pauraques flew, giving us a fleeting glance at this Mexican nightjar . . . another exciting new bird for our list.

Santa Ana has four photo blinds, each located at an active feeding station. Every morning during winter months, refuge personnel fill the sugar-water containers, replenish suet baskets and scatter seeds on the ground. Suddenly, birds are everywhere.

One hour in any of these photo blinds is well worth the visit to Santa Ana. Even if you don't have a camera, sit in the blind for superb close-up viewing of these exotic Mexican species. One blind is located on a pond used by black-bellied tree ducks, mottled ducks, cinnamon teal and least grebes.

The first experience we had in a photo blind was at the one called "Oriole" near Cattail Lake. Before we could set up our camera, we had a dozen plain chachalacas only 10 feet in front of us.

Then the green jays arrived. These brilliant blue-and-green birds don't look real to Northerners, who are accustomed to seeing much duller birds.

White-fronted doves waddled into the scene. They were

Above: A female hummingbird rested above a bed of flowers from which she gathered nectar just outside the headquarters door at Santa Ana.

Below left: Altamira (Lichtenstein's) orioles were frequent visitors to the sugar-water cup near Santa Ana headquarters.

Below right: A male golden-fronted woodpecker drank sugar water at a Santa Ana photo blind. The birds also relish the suet provided by refuge personnel.

The only clay-colored robin in the United States spent most of its time in this thicket at Santa Ana.

Another Mexican species, the ringed kingfisher, reaches the northern limit of its range at Santa Ana.

followed by Inca doves, curve-billed thrashers and a fat fox squirrel.

In the trees above this ground activity a Lichtenstein's oriole (also called Altamira or black-throated oriole) was dipping its long black bill into a sugar-water cup, and a golden-fronted woodpecker was pecking suet only 2 feet from the oriole. My problem was what to photograph first. In one hour, I shot over two hundred exposures.

The next day I watched a black-headed oriole drink sugar water at the feeder behind refuge headquarters. This bird was another new one for my life list.

Perhaps the highlight of our January visit to Santa Ana was a good look at the clay-colored robin, probably the only one in the United States at that time. This rare visitor from the other side of the Rio Grande looks much like our American robin except that it has pale gold on the breast and chocolate brown on the back. According to Wayne Shifflett, the clay-colored robin could almost always be found in the same tree overlooking the ponds where black-necked stilts, tropical kingbirds and great kiskadees (kiskadee flycatchers) feed. During our visit, there were also black skimmers on this pond, a rarity for Santa Ana.

Shifflett told us about a private pond to the east of the refuge where we found hundreds of black-bellied tree ducks, both species of night herons and our first look at a ringed kingfisher sporting a rufous breast and sitting on a wire over the pond.

Santa Ana and its neighbor refuge, Laguna Atascosa, take turns listing the greatest number of bird species found in any refuge in the National Wildlife Refuge system. At this writing they were even at 326. Santa Ana claims more species listed in the Fish and Wildlife Service's *Red Book* of endangered species than any other refuge in the system.

During our few days at Santa Ana, we saw 70 species, most of them new for the year, many of them new for our life lists.

LAGUNA ATASCOSA

The eager birder may be disappointed as he drives into Laguna Atascosa National Wildlife Refuge, especially if he has just come from Santa Ana, as we had. Unlike Santa Ana, at Laguna you must drive across 5 miles of very flat and uninteresting refuge terrain before arriving at the headquarters and good birding.

The day we arrived in late January, the wind was topping 30 mph. The barren, unplanted fields between the gate and the headquarters were foreboding and lacked any kind of birdlife. How could this wasteland claim to be one of the best bird refuges in the United States?

As we registered at the reception center, I never would have believed that in less than four hours, we would have recorded 66 species of birds. Until you actually pick up a tour map

Mistletoe grows in profusion in the low thickets of Laguna Atascosa.

and bird list and start driving the two tour roads through Laguna's different habitats, you have a hard time figuring out
where all the birds are.

It was only natural for us to compare Laguna Atascosa with
Santa Ana. They are only 60 miles apart, and both are located
near the Mexican border in the lower Rio Grande Valley. They
vie for being the top birding refuge in the National Wildlife
Refuge system, each with about 326 species. But in physical
appearance they are totally different. Santa Ana is a river-
bottom thicket which attracts song and upland bird species.
Laguna Atascosa is an open coastal prairie with salt flats and
low vegetated ridges supporting thick mesquite, ebony, huisa-
che, retama, granjeno, cacti and yucca. The area is bounded by
Laguna Madre Bay on the east and Laguna Atascosa Lake on
the west. Thus, Laguna is more of a waterfowl and water bird
area, with over 7,000 of its 45,190 acres in marsh and open
waters.

Laguna has two major auto tour routes: Lakeside and Bayside. Each is 18 miles long, and each takes about two hours
to cover.

Lakeside skirts Laguna Atascosa Lake, a 3,100-acre body of
fresh water for which the refuge is named. In January, this large
lake is normally covered with waterfowl, sometimes numbering
over a quarter million. On January 21, however, we saw only a
few hundred American coots, western grebes, canvasbacks and
gadwalls. Refuge personnel explained that a severe drought in
south Texas had caused most of the ducks to move farther south.

The Lakeside tour took us through the refuge's farmland,
where we saw Canada geese, sandhill cranes and white-tailed
deer. We also had our first look at a roadrunner.

The Bayside tour took us to the saltwater side of the refuge
and along the Laguna Madre Bay. This was famous until recently as the wintering waters for many of North America's
redheads. We saw only a few hundred of these ducks where
millions once floated. Because of the destruction of its nesting
habitat, the redhead has become another victim of man's reck-
less attitude toward the needs of wildlife.

Farther along the bay, we spotted the scarce white phase of
the reddish egret walking along the water's edge. We also

Perhaps the best place to see wildlife at Laguna Atascosa is at the World War II gunnery range where refuge personnel put out food for birds and other wildlife like these collared peccaries.

counted about 10 species of common ducks. In the short grassy fields leading to the water, we found Cassin's, seaside and savannah sparrows common. The Cassin's and seaside were life listers for Kit and me. A few flitted ahead of the car as we drove along. The strong wind picked them up and carried them ahead and quickly down again into the grasses, making identification more difficult. But persistence paid off.

Another good birding spot on the Bayside tour is the old World War II gunnery range at the beginning of the route. The concrete oval road is about all that is left of the range area, but that oval is one of the most remarkable feeding stations I've ever seen. Each day refuge personnel spread grain on the pavement, permitting an outstanding view of feeding songbirds and mammals.

We parked our station wagon on one side of the oval and waited. Through binoculars, we watched olive sparrows (another new one for our life list), long-billed and curve-billed thrashers, white-throated, song and savannah sparrows, mourning and white-fronted doves and a pack of collared peccaries, or javelinas. These little wild pigs are usually quite wary, but from the car we had a fine view of 7 as they came onto the concrete to eat grain.

Laguna also has photo blinds, one located on the oval at the gunnery range and one on a small lake nearby. We had heard that least grebes inhabited the small lake, so we walked the trail to the lake. The thickets along the trail were "wall-to-wall" mockingbirds all the way. The grebes were on the lake as predicted, right in front of the blind. Much to our surprise, a Cooper's hawk was also there. This raptor has become extremely scarce in recent years.

Our time at Laguna was all too short, but we were there long enough to learn why it is one of the star-spangled bird refuges. Like all the hot spots, Laguna has essential habitat in a critical location. Show me a birding hot spot and I'll show you a superb habitat in a strategic location.

VISITOR TIPS

Recommended time to visit: December through February.

Clothing: Light clothing will be in order most of the time. A few days were cool very early in the morning and we needed jackets. Remember your insect repellent for your visit to Aransas. All walking trails are beautifully maintained and easy to walk. Hiking boots are not necessary, but comfortable, sturdy walking shoes are.

Lodging: Near Aransas, Rockport and Port LaVaca have motels, as does Victoria, 50 miles from the refuge. For Santa Ana, the best bet is McAllen, although there may be something suitable for you in Alamo, San Juan or Pharr. Harlingen, Brownsville, San Benito and Port Isabel have motels in the Laguna Atascosa region.

Restaurants: Aransas: There are restaurants in Tivoli, including a good one serving Mexican food. Santa Ana: Many fine restaurants in McAllen, or cross the border into Reynosa for a real Mexican dinner. Laguna Atascosa: Restaurants can be found in Harlingen, Brownsville, Port Isabel and San Benito.

Camping: No camping is allowed in any of the three refuges. The nearest campground to Aransas is in Goose Island State Park, 30 miles to the south. Rockport has numerous campgrounds, and Port LaVaca, 35 miles to the north, has one. Or ask at refuge headquarters for directions to a privately owned camp halfway between the refuge and Austwell, which also has a few cabins. The closest campground to Santa Ana is at Bentsen/Rio Grande Valley State Park near Mission, Texas. Brownsville and Harlingen offer camping for Laguna Atascosa visitors.

Picnic Areas: Aransas: There are only two on the refuge—one near the Visitor Center and one just before the one-way road begins on the loop. At Santa Ana, the best place to eat a picnic lunch is along the loop road at Cattail Lake.

Reservations: The refuges were not being heavily used when we were there in January. But to be on the safe side, reservations for accommodations should probably be made about a week in advance. Write ahead for motel and camping information to:

> Laguna Atascosa:
> > Refuge Manager
> > 306 East Jackson Street
> > P.O. Box 2683
> > Harlingen, Texas 78550
> > (512) 423-8328

> Santa Ana:
> > Refuge Manager
> > Route 1, Box 202A
> > Alamo, Texas 78516

> Aransas:
> > Aransas National Wildlife Refuge
> > P.O. Box 68
> > Austwell, Texas 77950

Rest Rooms: In Aransas, rest rooms are located at the Visitor Center, the picnic areas and the observation tower. In Santa Ana they are at headquarters and at the picnic area. At Laguna Atascosa they are located near the registration area.

Telephone: Aransas: In Austwell or Tivoli. Santa Ana: Nearest public phone is in Alamo. Laguna Atascosa: Port Isabel.

Gasoline: Aransas: There are gas stations in Austwell, in Tivoli and on the road to Rockport. Santa Ana: You'll find gas along Highways 281 and 83 as well as all through McAllen. Laguna Atascosa: Port Isabel, Harlingen, San Benito, Brownsville.

Groceries: Aransas: Austwell, Tivoli and Rockport have grocery stores. Fresh shrimp and oysters can be had from a couple of places very close to the refuge. Ask for directions at headquarters. Santa Ana: McAllen and San Juan have grocery stores. Laguna Atascosa: San Benito, Port Isabel, Brownsville and Harlingen.

Hospital: Aransas: The nearest is in Port La Vaca. An ambulance will go as far as Tivoli. Santa Ana: McAllen. Laguna Atascosa: Brownsville.

Airport: Corpus Christi is the closest airport to Aransas. For Santa Ana and Laguna Atascosa the nearest airports are Brownsville and Harlingen.

Bird List: Bird checklists are available from the headquarters at all three refuges. Aransas' covers 328 species, Santa Ana lists 326 and Laguna Atascosa's includes 326 birds.

3

The Platte:

River of the Cranes

Neither the hordes of demoiselle cranes on the Nile nor the great flocks of European cranes at Oland in the Baltic can match the spectacle of the sandhill cranes, 225,000 strong, which use the Platte River as a staging area each March. It is the largest concentration of any species of crane, anywhere in the world.

—Roger Tory Peterson

There are only two species of cranes in North America—the whooping and the sandhill. The whooper is the world's rarest and the sandhill is the world's commonest crane.

We discovered that it is possible to see most of the world's wild population of whooping cranes in a single day (see chapter on southern Texas). We also found that it is possible to see most of the world's population of 250,000 sandhill cranes in a single day. The scene of this annual phenomenon is along the Platte River in central Nebraska in late March.

The 80-mile stretch of the Platte between Grand Island and Lexington and a 20-mile stretch of the North Platte River near Sutherland and Hershey are the main staging areas. As many as 225,000 sandhill cranes assembled there in late March consti-

In March, more than 200,000 sandhills "stage" along the Platte River in central Nebraska prior to their flights to as far away as Siberia.

Sandhill cranes are colored a delicate ash-gray except for their red cap. Legs and bill of the bird are gray-black, and a stylish pompadour on the crane's rump gives it a little flair.

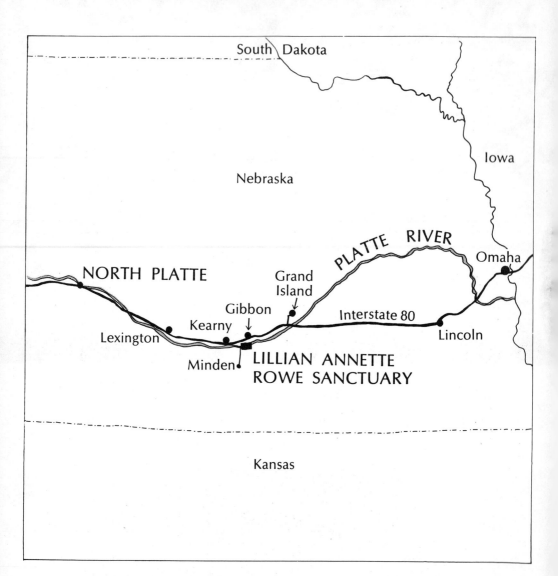

tute the largest concentration of any species of crane anywhere in the world.

Timing is essential at each of our hot spots, and Platte River is no exception. According to Ron Klataske, Regional Field Representative for the National Audubon Society, the peak period for the sandhills has traditionally been March 20 to 30.

I was in India from February 15 to March 19 on assign-

Described as a river a mile wide and an inch deep, the Platte affords a special combination of shallow water and numerous sandbars which is ideal habitat for roosting cranes.

ment for *International Wildlife* magazine. Instead of flying home to Milwaukee when I arrived back in the United States, I flew directly to Omaha, where Kit met me. She had fresh film, winter clothes and camping gear all ready to start our next adventure. What a shock Nebraska's icy winds were to my Indian suntan!

Our scheduling couldn't have been better. The Nebraska

Audubon Council was holding its annual crane meeting in Grand Island from March 20 to 22. By attending that meeting we were well oriented before venturing out to see the cranes for ourselves.

Among the interesting facts we learned at this meeting were:

1. That the staging area in central Nebraska is the narrow neck in an hourglass pattern the sandhills follow during migration. Most of the cranes winter in Mexico, Texas and New Mexico. In February they head for the Platte River, where they spend a month resting, feeding, courting and acclimating themselves for the rigorous flight north as far as northern Canada, Alaska and Siberia.

2. That the Fish and Wildlife Service was conducting a three-year study of cranes on the Platte River staging area, one phase of which was to determine the effects of hunting on the birds. (They are not hunted on the Platte.) In nine western states, including Alaska, the sandhills are hunted as game birds. The same is true in parts of Mexico, Canada and the Soviet Union.

3. That the National Audubon Society established an 1,800-acre crane sanctuary in 1973 in the name of a benefactor, Lillian Annette Rowe, near Gibbon, Nebraska.

4. That the Fish and Wildlife Service failed to gain landowner support for a proposed National Wildlife Refuge in 1974, but the Service was continuing its attempts to purchase parcels of land along the Platte River.

Following the meeting, we took to the road to see the cranes for ourselves.

It's not hard to find them. In fact, Ron Klataske claims that "it is impossible to stand in most areas along the Platte River during daylight hours between Grand Island and Lexington during the peak period without seeing sandhill cranes." The same can be said for Interstate 80 between those two communities, for the highway parallels the north side of the river and many of the cranes fly over the road.

We found that the best way to see the greatest number of cranes was to drive the secondary roads that parallel the river to the south. By keeping the big cottonwood trees that grow along

Sandhills grazing in the farm fields south of the Platte River rose in huge flocks as we drove past.

In zero weather, Kit and George Harrison huddled in a blind along the Platte to get photographs of the cranes coming in to the river to roost.

the river in sight, we were able to drive blacktops and gravel roads from Grand Island to Lexington. And did we see cranes! Thousands of them in the air, in cornfields, feeding, dancing, landing, taking off, in family groups, in huge flocks, flying at great altitudes, skimming the fields, coming from the river and going to the river . . . and all of them bugling.

Our routine was to spend the mornings and evenings in blinds next to the river. During the middle part of the day we were in the car, following the south side of the stream. If we wanted to make better driving time, we used I-80, but we saw and heard sandhills all the time, regardless of where we were.

The weatherman, however, was not our friend. In spite of the springlike weather the week before, our week in central Nebraska had only one day of clear sunny weather, and that was accompanied by 30-mph winds and temperatures in the mid-teens. Our many hours in the blind were, for the most part, very uncomfortable, but very worthwhile.

One evening was memorable because of the beautiful sunset we experienced. What a sight to see flock after flock of sandhills crossing the setting sun as they came in to the river to roost!

As we watched, the same question kept coming into our minds. What is it about the Platte River area that attracts 225,000 sandhills every spring? Why here? The answer lies in the unique habitat of the Platte River's shallow water and associated wet meadows. Apparently, there is no other place like it in North America that offers the cranes the kind of food and resting area they need en route to their breeding grounds.

Described as a river a mile wide and an inch deep, the Platte affords a special combination of shallow water and numerous sandbars that is ideal habitat for roosting cranes. To be able to stand in shallow water or on sandbars in an open river seems to give cranes a feeling of security. Less vulnerable there than in grassy meadows, sandhills congregate in the river just before dark and remain there until the sun begins to rise.

We found it hard to believe that there was enough food along the Platte at this time of the year to feed that many cranes. "To the contrary," reports Fish and Wildlife Service biologist Ray Buller. "In the cultivated fields there is an abundance of waste grain (mostly corn), and in the wet meadows that parallel the river there are frogs, crayfish, lizards, snakes, mice, insects, tubers, berries and weed seeds."

Jim Lewis, Assistant Unit Leader at the Oklahoma Cooperative Wildlife Research Unit, a crane expert, told us that these birds had been examined on their wintering grounds and they had very few fat deposits. Similar examinations on the Platte staging area showed a remarkable increase in fat on the same birds. Lewis explained that the birds need this staging area to prepare their bodies for both the flight to the breeding grounds and the nesting that follows. When the cranes arrive, the nesting grounds may be snow-covered and little or no food available. They must subsist on the fat they have acquired at the Platte.

When the birds first arrive on the Platte in late February, they find food easily in the fields closest to the river, but as the weeks pass and their numbers multiply, they must fly farther away from the river. When we were there, most of the birds were still within a couple of miles of the Platte. Klataske ad-

Sandhills congregated in the river just before dark and remained there until the sun began to rise. To be able to stand in the Platte's shallow water seemed to give them a sense of security.

Surprisingly nervous, the sandhills flushed in waves when cars or airplanes got too close.

vises visitors not to travel more than a few miles north of I-80 or more then 10 miles south of the river in search of cranes. "They seldom go beyond that distance and you're wasting your time if you drive farther," Klataske assured us.

Though they are easy to find in the fields south of the river, they are not as easy to approach as we were led to believe. When we spotted a large flock feeding in a cornfield ahead of us, the birds closest to the road flushed as we neared the field and either left the area or settled down much farther away. Without a telephoto lens, photography of these birds is difficult. The best one can hope for is a shot from the car of a great mass of birds rising in a flock. Aldo Leopold mentioned in *A Sand*

County Almanac that sandhill cranes are a symbol of wilderness and extremely wary of humans. We agree.

Another way to photograph them is from your own portable blind located along the river or near wet-meadow concentration areas. We visited the Lillian Annette Rowe Audubon Sanctuary for that purpose. You can reach the sanctuary by getting off at the Gibbon exit on I-80 and driving south about a mile to a dirt road. Drive west along the road for about 5 miles to the northern tract of the sanctuary.

The sanctuary consists of 4 contiguous miles of property on the north side of the river and about 1½ miles on the south side. Permission is required to enter the property. The Audubon warden, Bob Wicht, is listed in the Grand Island telephone directory. He is willing to conduct field trips and tours into the area, or allow observers to enter the sanctuary when it does not interfere with the natural behavior of the wary cranes.

Our best photography was done from blinds on the Audubon property. Bob Wicht was very generous in getting us into areas he felt were best for photography.

Each evening the cranes started arriving at the river by 6 P.M. (CDT). The light was still very good for photography. First the scouts landed and then took off again. Then small groups landed and remained. Most of the cranes landed on the sandbars and then waded into the shallow water. As the sun turned the western sky into a yellow-and-red backdrop, the number of cranes arriving in the river increased markedly. Just before the sun disappeared, the incoming crane traffic had reached a fever pitch. Some of the birds overshot the river, landing in the field beyond; others circled and then dropped onto the sandbars. The river was alive with bugling masses of cranes. *Nowhere* on the face of the earth can this sight be duplicated.

There are 6 subspecies of sandhill cranes. Three varieties, the Florida, Mississippi and Cuban cranes, are nonmigratory and listed as "rare" by the Fish and Wildlife Service. Fewer than 5,000 Florida and 200 Cuban and only 30 Mississippi cranes are known to exist.

The other three subspecies—the greater, the Canadian and the lesser sandhill cranes—are all migratory, and most pass through central Nebraska. On the Platte, 99 percent are lesser

Among the largest birds in North America, lesser sandhills have a 6-foot wingspan, stand 3½ feet tall and weigh up to ten pounds.

and Canadian. But estimates are that only 20,000 are Canadians. The balance are lesser sandhills.

The lessers are anything but small. They stand 3½ feet tall and weigh eight to ten pounds. Their wingspan is about 6 feet. Their coloring is a delicate ash-gray except for their red cap. The legs and bill of the bird are gray-black. The stylish pompadour on the crane's rump gives it a bit of flair.

Sandhills also have a fawn-colored wash on the wing, back and shoulder feathers. Apparently the iron-rich reddish soil found in parts of the cranes' range is responsible for this coloring. The birds have a habit of dipping their bills into the soil before preening their feathers, thus causing the stain. It is not clear why they do this. Some researchers believe it provides a cryptic coloration that helps camouflage the birds as they share incubation duties on the nesting grounds.

In addition to the sandhills staging from Grand Island to Lexington, there is another flock of 50,000 cranes on the North Platte near the community of North Platte. Including this westernmost flock, cranes can be found in late March nearly everywhere along the 150-mile stretch of the river and I-80 between Grand Island and Sutherland. Only the 19 miles between Odessa and Kearny are without cranes.

At the writing of this book, the cranes' staging area on the Platte was safe from any major threats of human intrusion or development, but encroachment in various forms continues along the banks of the Platte. As with so many rivers in America, its free-flowing character has also been threatened by the Government's dam-building agencies.

Perhaps the greatest threat to the river was a proposal called the Mid-State Reclamation Project. In 1970, conservationists and friends of the cranes began a fight against this $178-million Bureau of Reclamation irrigation project, maintaining that it was unnecessary. More than 95 percent of the land to be irrigated by this project, according to Klataske, was already under irrigation. Fortunately, a public referendum defeated the proposal. If the project had been allowed to go through, the Platte would have been dammed and channelized, and the vital habitat that attracts the migrating cranes would have been destroyed.

Continual draining of the wet meadows and the strip mining for gravel are eating away wet-meadow feeding grounds. A year before we arrived, the cranes had been feeding every day in a field now occupied by a truck-manufacturing company.

One can only speculate on the fate of the sandhill population if the Platte River staging area is gradually developed.

For more than ten million years the Platte has known the comings and goings of sandhill cranes. Individual birds have come there for as many as twenty springs. In less modern times, men felt a kinship with the river and its cranes. The arrival of the big gray birds marked the changing of the seasons. Now, men in steel machines race through the Platte country at 60 mph, heedless of this natural phenomenon so close to the interstate highway. But for those who still have a feeling for nature, the Platte River is the place to be in mid-March, where the trumpeting of the sandhills means that spring has come again.

VISITOR TIPS

Recommended time to visit: March 15 to 30.

Clothing: In March it is still winter in Nebraska. This means warm gloves, head covering and boots. If you're planning to put up a portable blind for photography or observation where you'll be stationary for several hours, you'd probably be most comfortable in a snowmobile suit.

Lodging: Accommodations can be found along Interstate 80 in the communities of Grand Island and Kearny.

Restaurants: There are several in Grand Island and Kearny.

Camping: Camping areas are easily accessible from I-80 at Mormon Island Recreation Park, near Grand Island, and at Wood River, Fort Kearny State Historical Park, Shelton Lake and Kearny County Recreation Area.

Picnic Areas: Picnic facilities are provided in all of the campgrounds mentioned.

Reservations: Really not necessary. Motels were practically empty during our visit. For motel and camping information, write ahead to:

> Grand Island Chamber of Commerce
> Grand Island, Nebraska 68801
>
> Robert J. Wicht, Warden
> National Audubon Society
> 2611 South Cochin Street
> Grand Island, Nebraska 68801
> (308) 382-3695

Rest Rooms: In the rest areas along I-80 or at the campgrounds.

Telephone: All the towns along I-80 have public telephones.

Gasoline: Easy to find, either along I-80 or in the towns along the highway.

Groceries: Grand Island and Kearny have a variety of supermarkets.

Hospital: Both Grand Island and Kearny have hospitals.

Airport: Lincoln, Nebraska, is the closest.

Bird List: There wasn't a printed one available at the time of our visit; we had to make our own.

4

Southeastern Arizona:
Rising from the Desert Floor

*When I first visited southeastern Arizona, they told me
that I would return. Its magnetic pull cannot be denied,
and I found myself going back to the same valleys, the
same canyons and the same mountains. Here one finds a
greater variety of nesting land birds than in any compa-
rable area in the United States. Like islands in the desert, the ranges of mountains have a family resemblance,
many things in common, but like islands, each one has
its own personality, its specialties not shared with its
neighbors.*

—*Roger Tory Peterson*

Like islands in a desert, the mountain ranges of southeastern
Arizona are isolated habitats which add up to one of the best
places in North America to see birds.

In these mountains—the Santa Catalinas, Santa Ritas, Huachucas and Chiricahuas—there are many canyons, lush with
vegetation, which birders find most rewarding.

A number of these have become world famous for the kinds
and numbers of birds they support. Their close proximity to
Mexico accounts for the fact that some species are found nowhere else in the United States.

The expression "If you've seen one, you've seen them all"
does not apply to the canyons of southeastern Arizona. Though
they do have certain wildlife and plant life in common, their

altitude, moisture and position in relation to the sun make each unique. Each has its own interesting bird populations.

But the canyons are only part of the reason southeastern Arizona is a hot spot. Each mountain range is surrounded by the Sonoran Desert, with dramatically different habitat and birdlife. This combination of desert and canyon birds is unique.

Because of the hot, arid climate, the desert birds tend to

With desert on all sides, Lower Sabino Canyon in the Santa Catalina Mountains is an oasis filled with old cottonwoods and teeming with birdlife.

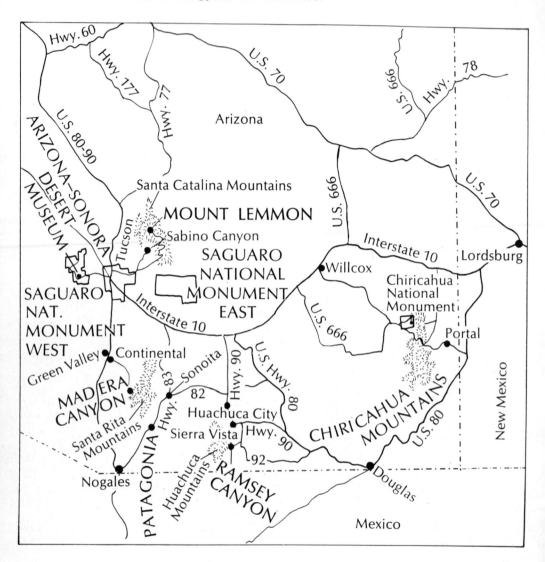

nest somewhat earlier than most others in North America. For this reason, we arrived in Tucson on April 29.

With the city as our first base of operations, we spent several days birding in Sabino Canyon, Mount Lemmon and Saguaro National Monument and at the Arizona–Sonora Desert Museum.

Our first stop was Sabino Canyon, 14 miles from the center of Tucson in the Santa Catalina Mountains. Sabino is a pretty little gorge nestled tightly into the dry desert mountains and lined with a stand of bright green cottonwood trees. The steep sides of the canyon are covered with huge saguaro cactus, acacia, cholla, prickly pear and palo verde, making Sabino a true desert oasis created by a fast-moving mountain stream.

On the map, it is called Sabino Canyon Recreation Area, a facility of the Coronado National Forest. To the nonbirding public, Sabino Canyon is better known as a picnicking area close to Tucson. And it was popular. By late morning, even during the week, the canyon was filled with young people, families and busloads of schoolchildren flocking to the area to picnic. But in desert country, the best birding is during early morning, so the picnickers did not inhibit the birders.

We found the best place to see birds was behind the dam in lower Sabino Canyon. The dam creates a broad stream bed shaded by a dense grove of old cottonwoods. On the days we were there, the cottonwoods were "snowing." The fluff was so deep in places that it created a cotton mist or fog as we waded through it, and the birds were almost as thick as the cotton fluff.

We were suddenly overwhelmed by both numbers and varieties of new birds and new songs. Familiar calls like those of cardinals sounded a little different and had to be checked. Our experience and how we sorted out the various species may be helpful to those readers who plan to visit Sabino Canyon. Don't be overwhelmed. Check each bird and birdsong until you can be sure of all the common ones. Then tackle those heard infrequently.

Our biggest problem was in identifying flycatchers. There were 12 different flycatchers on the Sabino Canyon bird list, and we had at least 4 singing at once: ash-throated, western, western wood pewee and western kingbird.

The most common and most raucous bird in Sabino, however, was Bell's vireo. There seemed to be a singing male every few feet.

Fortunately, we met Jeff and Bunkie Mangum of Tucson, who have been birding in Sabino for many years. In addition to helping us straighten out songs, they showed us nests of hummingbirds, Bell's vireos and a Cooper's hawk. The Bell's vireo nest was only 4 feet above the ground. It was a beautifully constructed cup containing four white eggs sparingly spotted. We heard and saw four warblers: Wilson's, MacGillivray's, Lucy's and yellow-rumped (Audubon's).

Early the next morning, Kit and I ate breakfast at the overlook in lower Sabino Canyon. The temperature was pleasant, the view was spectacular and the desert birds were everywhere. Gila woodpeckers, verdins, brown towhees, white-winged and mourning doves, cactus wrens and black-tailed gnatcatchers flitted around our table. One brown towhee turned out to be unusually tame. He ate scraps from a deep litter box provided by the Forest Service. When Kit took our breakfast scraps to the receptacle, the towhee was caught by surprise and the encounter scared both of them.

A stop at the Sabino Visitor Center for orientation, a bird list and a walk on its nature trail was productive. For people unfamiliar with desert plants, this nature trail is helpful in identifying common species. After May 1 the Visitor Center is closed for the summer because of the intense heat, and the operation is moved to the Palisades Ranger Station on the road to Mount Lemmon.

The following day we passed the ranger station en route to the top of 9,185-foot Mount Lemmon. The auto trip up the Santa Catalinas is a crash course in natural habitats. Starting at the desert floor, we drove through five life zones to the top of Mount Lemmon, where we found a Canadian-type forest. Each life zone had its own climate and its own plant and animal life.

To start this educational exercise, we drove out of Tucson on the Tanque Verde Road to Catalina Highway, which eventually became Hitchcock Highway. Then we drove 30 miles to the top of Mount Lemmon. The road is paved all the way.

As we approached the Santa Catalinas, we were driving through the Lower Sonoran Life Zone (up to 4,500 feet), where we found creosote, mesquite, acacia, palo verde and many cacti, including saguaros. We saw cactus wrens, gila woodpeckers, curve-billed thrashers, white-winged doves and roadrunners.

The Upper Sonoran Life Zone (4,000 to 7,500 feet) has three subzones: chapparal, oak woodland and piñon-juniper

We ate a most pleasant breakfast overlooking Lower Sabino Canyon while being entertained by a mixture of desert and canyon birds.

woodlands. At Molina Basin (4,300 feet) we were in oak-woodland vegetation and discovered our first bridled titmice. We also saw acorn woodpeckers, Mexican jays and brown towhees.

At 7,000 feet, the vegetation looked more like that of the northwestern United States. This was the Transition Zone (5,500 to 8,500 feet), where huge ponderosa pines dominated the terrain. Here we had our first view of yellow-eyed (Mexican) juncos. These tame little birds captivated us with their strange-looking eyes and unjuncolike walking gait. Other birds we saw in this zone were western and hepatic tanagers, black-headed grosbeaks, white-throated swifts and black-throated gray warblers.

As we approached the top of Mount Lemmon, we found patches of snow under white and Douglas firs. In this Canadian Life Zone (8,000 to 9,000 feet), the birds were characteristic of

Cactus wrens are well named. They spend most of their lives right in the cactus and even build their nests in a fortress of needles. This wren lived in Sabino Canyon.

habitats usually found much farther north: mountain chickadee, rufous-sided towhee and Steller's jay.

The University of Arizona has taken over an Air Force radar station on the summit and has installed an observatory. Unfortunately, the installation long ago destroyed the aesthetic beauty of this mountaintop. A ski resort one mile below has also scarred an otherwise beautiful pine/fir forest.

Nevertheless, the trip to the top of Mount Lemmon is an absolute *must* for every birder visiting southeast Arizona. In addition to the great variety of birdlife, the experience of passing from desert sands to deep snowbanks in only a few miles is an incredible one.

Another *must* stop in the Tucson area is the Arizona–Sonora Desert Museum, 14 miles west of Tucson over Gates Pass.

I had fond memories of Gates Pass and the museum from the summer 21 years earlier when I helped my father produce a film on the Sonoran Desert. As we drove over Gates Pass and down into Tucson Mountain Park, I was delighted to see that nothing had changed. Ahead of us lay perhaps the best desert garden in North America. The stands of giant saguaro alone make this area worth preserving. It was here, two decades earlier, that Dad and I drove to photograph blazing sunsets framed by the majestic saguaros.

Beyond Tucson Mountain Park, we passed Old Tucson, the Hollywood set for Western movies, and resisted a stop in our eagerness to get to the museum.

A living museum, with live animal displays, the Arizona–Sonora Desert Museum is world famous for its natural settings

One of the most popular living exhibits at the Arizona–Sonora Desert Museum is the grotto where the bobcat lives.

Kit made friends with a roadrunner at the Arizona–Sonora Desert Museum.

and avant-garde zoo concepts. Dedicated to showing only native species, the museum is a microcosm of life on the Sonoran Desert.

The walk-in bird display was our favorite, for inside we could get very close to and photograph many of the desert species. One particular roadrunner fell in love with Kit and presented her with flower blossoms, cigarette butts and dead leaves in return for gentle strokes on its back. The feeling of affection was mutual, and I had a hard time tearing Kit away.

Because the museum is an open-air facility, we saw wild desert birds like gila woodpeckers and curve-billed thrashers flying into displays such as the coatimundi den and the prairie dog village.

We ended that day afield at the Saguaro National Monument (West), which is near the museum. We found all the common desert species there and just outside the visitor center had our first look at black-throated sparrows.

The main attraction at the Saguaro National Monument, however, is the great stands of saguaros. The largest American cactus, the saguaro may reach a height of 50 feet and weigh up to 12 tons. An individual plant may live as long as 200 years, but getting started in life is very hazardous for young saguaros. They are susceptible to extreme temperatures, and for that reason, those which are sheltered by another plant are the ones which survive. Their growth rate for the first 10 to 15 years is very slow and they may reach only 6 inches in height. After this, however, with their root systems established, they grow rapidly. The tall saguaros provide nesting places for a number of birds such as gila woodpeckers, elf owls, mourning doves and red-tailed hawks.

From Tucson we moved south to Madera Canyon in the Santa Rita Mountains, located about halfway between Tucson and Nogales. We spent a pleasant three days in Madera with my parents, who were working on a western field guide to bird nests and eggs to be part of the Peterson Field Guide Series.

The principal attraction for Madera Canyon bird watchers is the coppery-tailed, or elegant, trogon. Estimated at only 12 to 15 nesting pairs in the United States, it is a rare bird by anyone's standards. There is some disagreement among bird watchers, however, as to the best place to see the trogon in Madera Canyon.

According to most of the literature, birders are directed up the Mount Wrightson and Josephine Saddle trails, which start from the upper parking lot. The brilliantly colored parrotlike birds were supposed to be nesting in holes in the sycamore trees in the upper canyon about one mile from where the trail begins.

Following what we took to be the best advice, we arrived at the upper parking lot soon after daylight on May 4 and took the trail marked "Mount Wrightson and Josephine Saddle." It was not until four hours and 3 miles later that we discovered we may have been on the wrong trail for the best chance of seeing a coppery-tailed trogon. The only binocular-clad hiker we met informed us that the other trail, unmarked and starting from the other end of the upper parking lot, was the only one from which he had seen the trogon in past years. In addition, on each of the three occasions he had seen the bird, it had been after late May.

Nevertheless, our search for the trogon up the Mount Wrightson–Josephine Saddle trail had been very rewarding in other ways. Without much difficulty, we spotted our first painted redstarts and red-faced, Townsend's and orange-crowned warblers, and we heard a Grace's warbler. We also recorded rufous-crowned sparrows, dusky-capped (olivaceous) flycatchers, Cassin's finches, western tanagers, Mexican jays, bridled titmice and verdins. The first painted redstart I saw came complete with a mouthful of nesting material. Fifteen minutes of patient watching led us to a beautiful grass-cup nest at the base of a tree on the steep hillside less than 20 feet from the path. A few days later, my father photographed it with eggs for his western field guide.

We saw the sycamore trees, many with holes in them, in which the coppery-tailed trogon was supposed to nest, but not the bird. At two locations we heard what sounded to us like the hen turkeys we had heard yelping many times in the woodlands of Pennsylvania. This is also a description for the call of the trogon, but we could not be sure of what we heard. There are turkeys in this area also.

Later in the week, we walked the other trail from the upper parking lot, but saw no coppery-tailed trogons there either. In fact, we knew of no sightings to date anywhere in the United States that spring. We did see yellow-eyed (Mexican) juncos, black-headed grosbeaks, gray-breasted (Mexican) jays, several hummingbirds and many Wilson's warblers. So it too was an excellent trail for birding, and we recommend both trails from the upper parking lot of Madera Canyon.

A sprinkling of wild bird seed on a nearby rock was so popular among the Madera Canyon gray-breasted Mexican jays that they fought over who would eat first.

The highlight of our days in Madera Canyon occurred at the Bog Springs Campground, where we made our home. On our second day, we noticed an elderly couple feeding hummingbirds in Campsite Number 7. We immediately became friends of Art and Frances Holmes of Bridgeton, New Jersey.

The Holmeses had been there for a week and were feeding red-tinted sugar water to at least 30 hummingbirds of 4 different species—black-chinned, broad-billed, broad-tailed and magnificent (Rivoli's). Using makeshift jars and glasses, plus a few "store-bought" feeders, the Holmeses had been entertained so much by the hummers that they had postponed leaving Madera for two days. Art is an experienced wildlife photographer. He had shot over two hundred color slides of hummers during their week in Madera Canyon and had some sage advice for me.

"Don't shoot your camera at ⅟125 of a second," Art said. "At that speed you don't see the wings at all. Shoot either faster or

Frances and Art Holmes of Bridgeton, New Jersey, spent a week at the Bog Springs Campground in Madera Canyon feeding and photographing hundreds of hummingbirds, orioles, tanagers and grosbeaks.

Frances Holmes held her finger still while her husband, Art, and the author photographed a male black-chinned hummingbird at the Bog Springs Campground in Madera Canyon.

slower. I always shoot at ⅕₀₀ of a second and stop most of the movement," Art concluded.

While Art manned his 35mm camera, Frances stood very patiently at the sugar water. When a hummingbird approached, she held out her finger for the hummer to use as a perch.

"That one didn't shut his engine down," Art explained, "but many of them will. They seem to love sitting on Frances' finger."

Though neither looked old enough, the Holmeses were celebrating their fiftieth wedding anniversary. They try to spend at least eight months of each year traveling in their camper. On this trip, they had left New Jersey the previous November.

We were the successors to Campsite Number 7 when the Holmeses left at noon on our second day. We took up the operation where Art and Frances had left off. Hummers were not the only birds attracted to the sweet water. We were hosts to black-headed grosbeaks, western tanagers (6 males at one time), Scott's and northern (Bullock's) orioles, bridled titmice, white-breasted nuthatches and gray-breasted (Mexican) jays. The nuthatches and jays ate peanut butter that we wedged into the tree bark.

Our days in Bog Springs Campground were as relaxed and pleasant as any in Arizona. What great entertainment to have all those birds around as we ate, worked, napped or just watched!

Before leaving Madera Canyon, we spent half a day in Florida Wash, a desert habitat along the road leading into Madera, about 8 miles from Continental. Here we found black-throated sparrows, curve-billed and crissal thrashers, both mourning and white-winged doves, Townsend's and Lucy's warblers, rufous-winged sparrows, verdins, Gambel's quail, white-necked ravens, cactus wrens and several species of hummingbirds.

No birding trip to southeast Arizona is complete without at least one day at Patagonia. A mixture of desert and canyon habitat, the Patagonia–Sonoita Creek Sanctuary is a facility of The Nature Conservancy. It straddles a meandering, cottonwood-shaded creek in the semiarid hills northeast of Nogales.

En route to Patagonia, we stopped to have a cup of coffee at one of the most famous roadside rest areas in the birding world.

Bridled titmouse.

A glass of sugar water attracted not only five species of hummingbirds but also these four songbirds to our campsite in Madera Canyon.

Western tanager.

Black-headed grosbeak.

Northern (Bullock's) oriole.

With the Santa Rita Mountains and Madera Canyon (center) in the distance, we found desert birding at its best in Florida Wash (foreground).

It is located 14 miles from Nogales on Route 82, just before you reach Patagonia. It too is on Sonoita Creek.

It is here, in the large sycamores over or near the roadside picnic tables, that the rare rose-breasted becards nest annually. (In the last few years they have nested up the road or across the creek.) Across the highway and beyond the creek, five-striped sparrows are fairly common in summer. Apparently we were too early for either. We found band-tailed pigeons, hooded orioles, brown-headed cowbirds, brown towhees, Bell's vireos, white-winged doves and cardinals very common in the roadside rest area.

Continuing on Route 82 one mile toward Patagonia, we turned left on a dirt road and doubled back sharply along the highway and then forded Sonoita Creek. We were on Salero Road, which is the most interesting route to the sanctuary.

Immediately after we forded Sonoita Creek, we stopped in a wooded grove to get a good look at our first vermilion fly-catcher. From that point on, the brilliantly colored flycatchers and their duller-colored relatives, the Cassin's kingbirds, were plentiful. We found violet-green swallows along this road as well as a black phoebe and a pair of summer tanagers.

The sanctuary is well marked and can be entered through any of four walk-in gates. The four areas are contiguous, but we found it more convenient to explore a section at a time and then drive on to the next one.

Although the habitat in the four areas is generally the same, we saw different kinds of birds in each location. The entire sanctuary was filled with birds, but noteworthy were the nesting black hawks, black phoebes (two nests) and Lucy's, yellow-rumped (Audubon's), MacGillivray's and hermit warblers—the last two undoubtedly being migrants. We also saw yellow-throats, yellow-breasted chats, hermit thrushes and gray hawks (another life lister).

I commend The Nature Conservancy for saving the area, but I was disturbed by the condition of Sonoita Creek. Apparently it is an open sewer for the little community of Patagonia, because it smelled terrible and was strewn with debris. This was the only discordant note we had for an area that we rank very high as a birding hot spot in southeast Arizona.

From Patagonia, we moved on to the Huachuca Mountains and famous Ramsey Canyon, about 6 miles south of Sierra Vista and the U.S. Army's Fort Huachuca.

Ramsey is a short and narrow canyon compared with Madera, but to many birders it is the hummingbird capital of the United States.

Birders who visit Ramsey stop or stay at Mile-Hi Ranch, which was recently purchased by The Nature Conservancy and caters to people interested in birds. I had never seen such a display of hummingbird feeders. Each little cabin had its own string of a half dozen or more. The management fills the feeders every few hours, and the birds consume about two gallons of sugar water a day!

On our afternoon there, we photographed a great many hummingbirds. During the year, Mile-Hi feeds 12 different

Ramsey Canyon, in the Huachuca Mountains, is called the "hummingbird capital of the world." We found five species of hummers there the day we visited.

A bright red house finch savored the sugar water at Mile-Hi Ranch in Ramsey Canyon.

Wheeling in a great circle, the roseate spoonbill set its wings for a landing in a nearby Everglades mangrove.

Mexican species, like this striking green jay, fed without fear only a few feet in front of our photo blind at Santa Ana.

When 225,000 sandhill cranes assemble on the Platte River in March, they constitute the largest concentration of cranes in the world.

Tired and hungry scarlet tanagers at Point Pelee National Park paid no attention to us as we photographed them through short lenses.

One of four species of hummingbirds attracted to our campsite in Madera Canyon, this broad-billed male enjoyed a mixture of sugar water.

With the grace of a ballerina, this avocet carefully moved toward its nest and eggs in the Bear River Migratory Bird Refuge.

A few feet outside our blind at Machias Seal Island, a puffin landed on the rock just above its nest. For us, a dream had come true.

Hawk Mountain's North Lookout is the place to see more hawks in a single day than most people see in a lifetime.

Navigating along the Atlantic Coast, migrating birds like these black skimmers and short-billed dowitchers back up at Cape May Point before striking out over Delaware Bay.

Bonaventure Island, at the point of the Gaspé Peninsula, is home to 18,000 pairs of gannets, the largest gannetry in North America.

With Mount Shasta as a backdrop and Tule Lake's masses of waterfowl as a foreground, you have a scene such as our early explorers described.

There are more Canada geese at Horicon—200,000 or more each year—than have ever before gathered in one place on the North American continent.

species, but there were only 5 species present on May 6: black-chinned, broad-billed, broad-tailed, magnificent (Rivoli's) and a new one for us, the blue-throated. The feeders are also used by many other birds, including painted redstarts, a surprise to us.

The drive to and from Ramsey also produced some new birds for the list. North of Nogales, past Patagonia on Route 82 near the little crossroads of Sonoita, we found ourselves in the heart of cattle country with grassy plains on both sides of the road. Strangely, here we saw eastern meadowlarks, lark sparrows and horned larks.

Many birders consider the Chiricahua Mountains, in the extreme southeast corner of Arizona, to be the best birding spot in the United States. The drive from Tucson to Portal takes about 3½ hours. We crossed into New Mexico on Interstate 10 and then back into Arizona on Route 80.

Many birders consider the Chiricahua Mountains, in the extreme southeast corner of Arizona, the best birding spot in the United States.

Portal is a crossroads at the east entrance to the Chiricahua section of the Coronado National Forest. We found the scenery here breathtaking, certainly the finest we had seen in Arizona. The stalwart red cliffs, pockmarked with countless caves and crevices, gave us the feeling that this was truly Apache country. Here white-throated swifts vie with prairie falcons in spectacular aerial displays, while on the outer walls facing the eastern desert, golden eagles have undisputed mastery of the air.

Our first stop was at the South Fork Campground in Cave Creek Canyon. We were again on the trail of the coppery-tailed trogon. This is supposed to be one of the best places in the United States to see the bird, but after an hour of hunting we

At the Southwest Research Station of the American Museum of Natural History we found another active sugar-water feeder which attracted western tanagers, black-headed grosbeaks and four species of hummingbirds, including this blue-throated.

gave up and drove to the Southwest Research Station of the American Museum of Natural History to inquire about where to look.

We were politely told that it was too early. No trogons had yet been reported. The end of May would be better. But we did enjoy the sugar-water feeders on the Research Station grounds. Black-headed grosbeaks and Scott's orioles, house finches and the usual hummingbirds, including the blue-throated, fed heavily. Say's phoebes caught insects near the feeders.

Our next stop was to be Rustler's Park, 10 miles ahead. But by the time we left the Research Station, we decided that the Rustler's Park Campground might be too high and too cold at that time of the year for comfortable sleeping. So, fortunately, we drove back to Cave Creek Canyon and the South Fork Campground.

There were two other cars in the camp, one from Illinois and one from Michigan, but no people around. After selecting a site along the dry creek bed, we began to set up our tent and kitchen.

Suddenly I heard a strange call that sounded like an owl's. It was 6:15 P.M., and I figured that an owl must have been getting an early start on his nightly serenade.

The call seemed close, and I looked up into the sycamores to see if I could spot the bird. On first glance, I saw a red spot. A large, bright red spot—a red breast. Too large to be a painted redstart . . . long tail. "My God . . . it's a . . . it's a . . . my God, Kit, it's a coppery-tailed trogon!"

Both of us stood spellbound. The bird was only 60 feet away in a sycamore on the opposite side of the creek bed. Even without binoculars, we could see his raspberry-red breast, long tail and distinctively marked head. With binoculars, it was unbelievable!

The male trogon flew about 10 feet to another sycamore that had a hole in it. He seemed to be examining the hole as a possible nesting site. Then he flew even closer to us, this time facing away, so we could see his iridescent green back and coppery tail.

His calls were now clearly like that of a hen turkey calling four or five soft yelps. The only difference between the trogon's

Above this picnic table we recorded the first U.S. sighting for the year of the elegant (coppery-tailed) trogon. What a great moment that was!

call and those of the turkeys I have heard was that the trogon's was a little deeper, softer and more hoarse. Perhaps an "oink, oink" instead of a turkey's "took, took" is a better description. It did sound somewhat like the calls we had heard earlier in Madera Canyon.

Our friend stayed around the campsite for about 10 minutes and then disappeared. At that hour, it was too dark for photographs.

On the back window of the Illinois car in the next campsite was a sign, "Bird Watcher." The occupant was off looking for birds (perhaps the coppery-tailed trogon) at the time. Had he only stayed in his camp, he would have seen one of the most sought-after, most exotic and rarest birds in the United States.

At 5:30 the next morning, we were awakened by the now familiar trogon call. He was back! Emerging sleepy but excited from our tent, we were rewarded by an even better look. This time he was only 20 feet above our picnic table. Again there was not enough light for photographs. He stayed with us another 10 minutes and again disappeared.

The Illinois bird watcher in the adjacent campsite was still in his sleeping bag!

On our way out of the canyon, we stopped at the ranger station to report our discovery. The Forest Service personnel were delighted to know that the trogons were back from their wintering grounds in Mexico. Ours was the first sighting that year in the Chiricahuas and probably in the United States. We heard from Dad that no one saw a trogon in Madera Canyon until nearly two weeks later.

Normally, male trogons are seen at the South Fork Campground by mid-April, but this year they were late.

There are only 8 trogons known to summer in the Chiricahuas, a few more in the Santa Ritas and the Huachucas. A total of perhaps 12 to 15 pairs breed in southeastern Arizona, and nowhere else in the United States. The only record of a trogon wintering in the United States was in Madera Canyon during the winter of 1973–74.

We were told that the trogons like people and continue to nest in the campground at South Fork despite the harassment they endure from eager bird photographers and others trying to get a closer look.

From Cave Creek, we drove to the top of the Chiricahuas on a primitive dirt road through Onion Saddle and Rustler's Park. The drive reminded us a little of Mount Lemmon as we passed through the oak-juniper belt to the ponderosa pines area at 8,500 feet in Rustler's Park. Yellow-eyed (Mexican) juncos, Grace's warblers, solitary vireos, western and hepatic tanagers, pygmy nuthatches, purple martins, Steller's jays and Townsend's solitaires were seen along the road and in Rustler's Park.

Though a bit cool, the campground area was beautiful and quiet, and it smelled of pines. If we had not been pressed for time, we would have spent a day of two in Rustler's Park.

On our trip down the west side of the Chiricahuas we stopped at the Pinery Canyon Campground, where we saw gray-sided (Mexican) chickadees and hermit thrushes.

On the west side of the mountains, we stopped for lunch at the Chiricahua National Monument. The campgrounds there had fearless black-headed grosbeaks, gray-breasted (Mexican) jays, white-breasted nuthatches and acorn woodpeckers, all of which gratefully accepted handouts from picnickers and campers.

Our time in Arizona was running out. We had to make a plane in Salt Lake City for Point Pelee in two days, and we reluctantly left the Chiricahuas and headed for Utah.

VISITOR TIPS

Recommended time to visit: May 1 to June 15.

Clothing: The clothes we packed for Arizona ran the gamut from summer shorts to down jackets—and we needed all of it! Around Tucson it was always hot during the day. Evenings were warm, and only a light sweater was occasionally needed. Nights and early mornings in the canyons were cold. When we crawled out of our sleeping bags before dawn, we snuggled into our down jackets, and as the morning wore on we peeled off layer after layer until by midmorning we were in very lightweight summer clothing. To put it briefly, pack so you're prepared for temperatures ranging from about 40° to 90° F.

Lodging: If you're birding in the Santa Catalina area—Mount Lemmon, Sabino Canyon, Saguaro National Monument, Arizona–Sonora Desert Museum—you have the whole city of Tucson from which to choose. The Santa Rita Lodge in Madera Canyon and the Mile-Hi Ranch in Ramsey Canyon both cater to birders, and both have housekeeping units. You should have a reservation well in advance if you're considering one of these, because both are very popular among bird watchers. Sierra Vista is another good place to find lodging in the Ramsey Canyon vicinity. For Patagonia, you can choose from several fine modern motels in Nogales or a recently constructed motel in Patagonia just a half mile from the Patagonia–Sonoita Creek Sanctuary. There is also a guest ranch located near the famous roadside rest area. In the Chiricahuas, Portal has two lodges with cooking facilities. Douglas and Lordsburg also have motels.

Restaurants: Tucson again for Mount Lemmon, Sabino Canyon, Saguaro National Monument and the Arizona–Sonora Desert Museum. If you're in Madera Canyon, the Santa Rita Lodge has an excellent restaurant, or take a thirty-minute drive into Green Valley. In Ramsey Canyon, the nearest dining facilities are in Sierra Vista. There is no restaurant at Mile-Hi; they feed only the birds. In the Patagonia area, Nogales is your best bet. If you're looking for a dining-out spot in the Chiricahuas, you'll have quite a drive to either Douglas or Lordsburg . . . better pack some food.

Camping: There are dozens of campgrounds in the Tucson area, some commercial and some maintained by the U. S. Forest Service. The ones we passed on the road to the top of Mount Lemmon were especially scenic and well maintained. We stayed at the Tucson Holiday Inn Trav-L-Park to be centrally located. In Madera Canyon, the Bog Springs Campground is really the only one in the area. It's a popular spot, particularly on weekends, so get there early to be certain of having a campsite. The closest campground to Ramsey at the time we visited was at Parker Canyon Lake. There are no campgrounds in Patagonia. If you're camping, you'll probably do best to stay in Madera Canyon, as we did, and drive to Patagonia from there. You'll find several campgrounds through the Chiricahuas from Portal to the Chiricahua National Monument, all with spectacular scenery.

Picnic Areas: You'll never have trouble finding an interesting place to picnic in southeastern Arizona. There are pleasant picnic areas in or near all of our Arizona birding hot spots.

Reservations: Reservations should be made about three to four weeks in advance except as noted below. Write ahead for motel and camping information to:

> Tucson Chamber of Commerce
> Tucson, Arizona 85700

> Nogales Chamber of Commerce
> Nogales, Arizona 85621

> Santa Rita Lodge
> Box 444
> Amado, Arizona 85640
> (602) 625-8746
> (Make reservations at least four months in advance)

> Mile-Hi Ranch
> Hereford, Arizona 85615
> (602) 378-2785
> (Make reservations three to four months in advance)

For camping sites in Madera Canyon, the Chiricahuas, Mount Lemmon, Sabino Canyon, contact:

> Supervisor, Coronado National Forest
> Federal Building
> Tucson, Arizona 85701

Rest Rooms: No problem in any of the Tucson-area spots. In Madera Canyon, the campground has rest rooms. There are no public facilities either at Patagonia or at Mile-Hi Ranch in Ramsey Canyon. The Chiricahua route has several along the way in campgrounds, as well as at the Chiricahua National Monument Headquarters and Visitor Center.

Telephone: Public phones are everywhere in Tucson. In Madera Canyon there is one outside the Santa Rita Lodge. None at Mile-Hi, but in an emergency, you might ask to use a private phone. The nearest one to the Patagonia–Sonoita Creek Sanctuary is in Patagonia. In the Chiricahuas, we didn't see a public phone, but if an emergency should arise in which you need a telephone, go to the ranger station or the Chiricahua National Monument Visitor Center.

Gasoline: It's available in Tucson, Green Valley and Continental, near Madera Canyon; the Sierra Vista area near Ramsey Canyon; in Patagonia and in Nogales. In the Chiricahuas, Willcox, Douglas and Lordsburg have gas stations.

Groceries: Tucson, again, in the Santa Catalina birding spots. Continental, near Madera Canyon, has a small general store, and Green Valley has several modern supermarkets. In the Patagonia area, shop in Nogales or in Patagonia. Ramsey Canyon's nearest food stores are in the Sierra Vista/Huachuca City region. Get groceries at Portal (a small store), Willcox, Douglas or Lordsburg in the Chiricahuas.

Hospital: Tucson and Nogales have hospitals.

Airport: Tucson.

Bird List: Checklists are available at the Visitor Centers in Sabino Canyon (116 species listed) and in the Chiricahua National Monument (167 species), at Mile-Hi Ranch (239 species) and at Santa Rita Lodge (170 species). A checklist of the birds of southeastern Arizona may be obtained (15 for $1) from L & P Photography, Box 19401, Denver, Colorado 80219.

5

Point Pelee:
Funnel to the North

No other spot in the interior of the continent can offer the bird lister more action on a good day in May or in September. Funneled into the long finger of land that probes Lake Erie, thousands of small migrants enliven the woods and thickets. No other vantage point in the Great Lakes region has produced as many rarities.

—*Roger Tory Peterson*

If you are a bird lister, as we are, and if you get a charge out of running up a big total of birds seen in a single day or on a field trip, as we do, then give yourself a special treat. Go to Point Pelee National Park, Ontario, in mid-May. It's a bird lister's paradise.

Birds arrive at Point Pelee in such numbers of species and in such large flocks of the same species that some people find the phenomenon unbelievable when seen for the first time.

One of the biggest days in the history of bird watching at Point Pelee was May 11, 1963. Individual birders totaled 143 species, and some claimed as many as 150. That day was exceptional, but officials at Point Pelee told us that on an average day in mid-May, birders can easily see 50 to 75 species, sometimes 100.

The point of Point Pelee is the southernmost tip of mainland Canada. Hundreds of species of birds arriving after a long flight over Lake Erie must rest and feed before continuing their migration north.

Why is Point Pelee National Park one of the hottest places in North America for bird watching? Like all the birding hot spots in this book, the answer is geography, habitat and timing, but at Point Pelee, the geography and the timing are dramatic.

Point Pelee is a peninsula that juts into Lake Erie, making it the southernmost tip of mainland Canada. This 6-square-mile

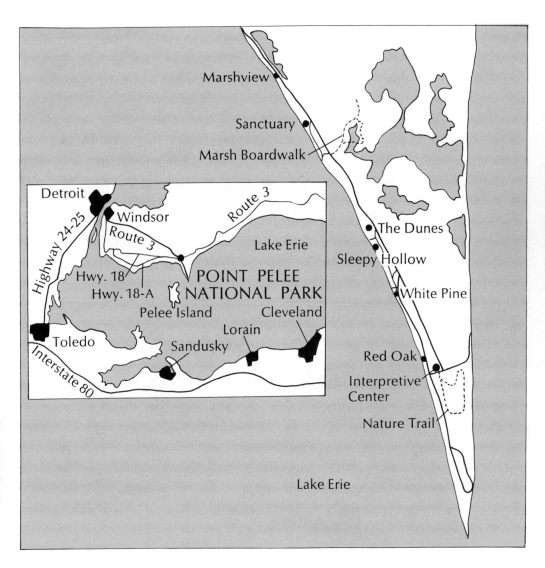

area of marsh, beach and deciduous forest is a significant landmark in the north–south migration routes of two major bird
flyways. Birds flying north in the spring leapfrog from Ohio to
the two Canadian islands of Pelee and Middle and finally to
Point Pelee on the Canadian mainland, where they arrive tired
and hungry. In the fall, southward-moving flocks of birds back

Early-morning birders at the tip of Point Pelee searched for new species that had arrived overnight.

Waves of warblers and scores of other species passed through the woodlands of Point Pelee National Park as eager bird watchers added to their daily lists.

up on Point Pelee waiting for favorable weather conditions before making the big push over the lake.

Weather is the controlling factor for both spring and autumn flights. Some years when storms and weather fronts are common, the waves of birds are spectacular. Other years, weather conditions control a more subtle flow which is disappointing to expectant bird watchers.

"On a good day," reported Brian Morin, resident ornithologist at Point Pelee, "it is possible to have a total of 200 species counted by all birders in the park and close to a million birds seen."

Records show that different days will bring different birds. There have been "big days" for whistling swans, 650; red-breasted mergansers, 6,000; whimbrels (Hudsonian curlews), 250; flickers, 250; barn swallows, 1,000; white-throated sparrows, 20,000, and ruby-throated hummingbirds, 200. Since 1877, a total of 336 species has been recorded.

"On May 22, 1974, there were large numbers of people in the park," Morin recalls. "At 7 A.M., a group of fifteen to twenty birders standing on the tip of the point without moving counted 23 species of warblers.

"I also remember a day in late May, 1972," Morin continued. "I was alone on the tip for about an hour and a half. During that time I saw a bobwhite, a prothonotary warbler, both little and Franklin's gulls, a western kingbird and a magpie. I finally had to find another birder to share this with."

The reason a wave of birds descends on the Point during any particular day or night is not fully understood. According to Dr. George M. Stirrett, former Chief Naturalist of Canada's national parks and author of a series of booklets on the birds of Point Pelee, it appears to be the result of a warm weather front advancing from the southeast meeting a cold front coming from the northwest.

Stirrett claims that two situations will cause birds to descend in large numbers: "One is when the two fronts meet at ground level. The other is when a warm front in which migrating birds are flying overrides a cold front. The warm air becomes cooler as it rises and is finally too cold for the birds, and they descend."

Exhausted and hungry birds on the beach at the tip of Point Pelee were easy to approach and photograph.

Waves of migrants often bring rarities—such as the chuck-will's-widow, mountain bluebird and worm-eating and Virginia warbler, as well as the scarlet ibis, American avocet, lark bunting, lesser nighthawk, summer tanager, northern (American) three-toed woodpecker and a black-legged kittiwake, to mention a few.

When birds are grounded at Point Pelee during a storm, they are often so exhausted that they can be approached easily. Some of the smaller birds have actually alighted on people standing at the tip of the point.

Then there is sometimes a "visual reverse migration" in which birds appear to be flying south and sometimes fly back over the lake to the United States during a spring flight.

"Reverse migration is not always related to weather," theorized Morin. "This phenomenon may be caused by a disorientation when birds have crossed Lake Erie farther east and followed the Canadian shoreline west. They find themselves on the tip of Point Pelee heading south again. But they eventually get straightened out and come back across later."

When Kit and I arrived at Point Pelee on May 11, there were no storm systems or approaching fronts in the weather forecast. This worried us. However, we found Point Pelee teeming with birds. In the first two hours, we counted 49 species; in the first two days we tallied 115. During our three days at Point Pelee, all observers in the park recorded a combined total of 191 different species. No doubt about it, Point Pelee is one of the best places in North America to run up a bird list in a hurry.

Our first dinner in the White Pine picnic area was a revelation in itself. From our table, we saw 11 different species of warblers between 5 and 6 P.M. During that same hour we also recorded red-headed and red-bellied woodpeckers, gray catbirds, red-breasted nuthatches, blue jays, common crows, 4 thrushes (hermit, Swainson's or olive-backed, gray-cheeked and American robin), ring-necked pheasants, white-throated sparrows (everywhere) and white-crowned sparrows, northern (Baltimore) orioles and others.

On the next evening at Sleepy Hollow picnic area, the trees above the table were filled with Cape May, Nashville, black-and-white and magnolia warblers—hundreds of them.

The highlight of each day, however, was the dawn trek to the tip of the peninsula to see what new birds had arrived during the night.

This daily ritual is attended by only the most dedicated bird watchers, who answer a 5 A.M. alarm, dress hurriedly and dash to the Interpretive Center before 6 to meet the "train" that they hope will carry them the 1½ miles to the tip of the peninsula. (It runs that early only when thirty or more people sign up for it. Cars are banned from the tip from April 1 to Labor Day.) We were lucky. More than thirty people were there each morning. Upon detraining 1,000 yards from the tip, we joined the crowd of binocular-clad, tripod-equipped, camera-laden ornithologists who made their way en masse to the tiny spit of land curving out into the waters of Lake Erie.

"Lot of ringbills out there, but can't find a herring. No little gull, either."

"That's a black-throated blue female. See the white check on its wing."

An indication of the density of migrating birds were these three species of thrushes—veery, hermit and Swainson's (olive-backed)—feeding together on the road to the tip of Point Pelee.

The most common songbird at Point Pelee while we were there was the white-throated sparrow.

A wave of rose-breasted grosbeaks surged through Point Pelee on our second day in the park.

A water pipit searched the gravel shores of Lake Erie for food after its long flight to Point Pelee.

During migration periods, the point of Point Pelee is closed to auto traffic. Those who don't want to walk the 1½ miles to the tip may ride on this "train" leaving every half hour.

"I guess you have the Carolina wren, don't you?"

"Oh, yes, there are so many of them."

"What do you have over there?"

"A water pipit . . . on that log."

"A water pipit! Where?"

"Wow! That chestnut-sided warbler almost hit me. I guess he's not too alert either this morning."

"That bird up there looks like a red-eyed vireo."

"Are you sure?"

"Yeah, it has definite head markings. I'll put the scope on him for you. Oops, forget it. He's gone."

Our mornings at the tip were great. It was really a memorable experience to see deep-woods warblers like the Blackburnian feeding on insects on a sand beach. I had never been so close to chestnut-sided, yellow-rumped (myrtle) or Nashville warblers. Being able to fill the camera frame with the Philadelphia vireo was an exciting experience. Scarlet tanagers allowed me to shoot close-up photographs by merely walking up to them. At times the brilliant red birds were too close for me to focus the telephoto lens I was carrying. What a complaint!

On another morning at the tip, as we were watching our first little gulls, we saw 12 Bonaparte gulls knock a blue jay into the water. The jay struggled 300 feet to the shore and escaped. A few days earlier, ring-billed gulls attacked a grackle over the water and killed it. Strangely, none of the gulls could carry the dead grackle to the shore, and they didn't want to eat it in the water.

The tip of the peninsula is not the only hot spot in Point Pelee's 6-square-mile area. The marshland on the northeast side of the point is also a great place to bird. Park people have built a ⅔-mile-long boardwalk, a third of it floating on the marsh, with observation stations for looking out over the 2,400-acre wetland. Here we saw long-billed marsh wrens, American bitterns, common yellowthroats and many red-winged blackbirds. A least bittern had been seen there the previous night.

Marsh wrens, bitterns, yellowthroats and other species can easily be seen and heard from the floating boardwalk, two-thirds of a mile long, at Point Pelee.

The 1¼-mile nature trail beginning and ending at the Point Pelee Interpretive Center is one of the best we have ever walked. It traverses several different habitats, including this wet woodland with upturned tree roots.

The best nature trail I've ever walked is the 1¼-mile trail starting and ending at the Interpretive Center. The path took us through several different habitats, including a wet woodland with turned-up tree roots and moss-covered logs—ideal habitat for prothonotary warblers, northern waterthrushes and winter wrens. Rose-breasted grosbeaks were extremely tame along this trail. In one tree, we spotted 3 Cape May warblers, 4 northern (Baltimore) orioles and a red-headed woodpecker. It looked like a decorated Christmas tree.

No matter where we were those three days at Point Pelee, birds were everywhere . . . in every tree, every bush, every brush pile. Strange combinations of birds such as great (formerly American or common) egrets overhead and scarlet tanagers in front of us; little gulls on one side and Blackburnian warblers on the other; red-winged blackbirds sharing trees with magnolia warblers; water pipits with flickers; orchard orioles with red-breasted mergansers; indigo buntings with black-bellied plovers. Migration time at Point Pelee makes strange "birdfellows."

Spring is not the only time to see migrating birds at Point Pelee. Brian Morin described to us how the fall migrants back up on Pelee waiting for favorable weather before crossing the lake.

"Spring has its rarities, fall has concentrations," said Morin, who had spent five years at Point Pelee as a Seasonal Naturalist.

"You can count 100,000 common terns here in mid to late autumn. Also a thousand sharp-shinned hawks in a day," Morin stated.

But spring is the time when Pelee attracts the greatest number of bird species and the greatest number of bird watchers. On an average weekend, at least five hundred people come to the park to see the spring show. Forty or more usually show up each morning for the train ride to the tip.

Having just returned from ten days in southeastern Arizona with what we thought was a big list (124 species), we were amazed to come close to matching that number with 115 in only two days at Point Pelee. The following weekend, the American Birding Association held its annual meeting at Point Pelee and recorded 212 species during four days of observation. No question about it, Point Pelee is the place in eastern North America to see a great many different kinds of birds in a very short period of time.

VISITOR TIPS

Recommended time to visit: For peak spring migrations, the second and third weeks of May.

Clothing: Those early mornings at the tip are cold, damp and windy. You'll need to dress warmly for the dawn rites, but by midday you'll need only a light jacket or sweater. Many birders wore lightweight

Blackburnian warbler.   Red-breasted nuthatch.

It was a strange experience to see these tired and hungry birds of the deep woodland feeding on the beach insects at the tip of Point Pelee.

Magnolia warbler.

Chestnut-sided warbler.

Philadelphia vireo.

pull-on rubber boots to keep the sand out of their shoes while they were traipsing out to the tip.

Lodging: Accommodations are available in Leamington, within minutes of the park gate.

Restaurants: There are restaurants in Leamington. We saw mobile snack trailers in the park, but they were not in operation at that time of the year.

Camping: There is none in the park except for group camping. A campground with showers is located within 2 miles of the park entrance.

Picnic Areas: There are several areas along the park road, and every one is beautiful. They are at Marshview, The Dunes, Sleepy Hollow, White Pines and Red Oak.

Reservations: Write ahead for motel and camping information to:

> Point Pelee National Park
> Leamington, Ontario N8H 3V4
> (519) 326-3204

Rest Rooms: At all the picnic areas, at the beaches and in the interpretive center.

Telephone: Public phones are located at the headquarters building, at the bathhouse near the tip and in Leamington.

Gasoline: Available in Leamington and also on the road to the park.

Groceries: Available throughout Leamington as well as along the road to the park.

Hospital: In Leamington.

Airport: Windsor, Ontario, is the closest.

Bird List: Checklists of 318 species may be obtained at the Point Pelee Interpretive Center.

6

Bear River:

Paradise for Water Birds

More than a century ago when Jim Bridger paddled his buffalo-skin boat through the gorge of Bear River where the stream meanders across the sprawling delta marshland before pouring its fresh mountain water into Great Salt Lake, the sky was darkened by a million wings. Today as we drive out along the broad dikes which impound the water at the mouth of the Bear River, it is again possible, as it was in Jim Bridger's day, to see a million blackbirds.

—*Roger Tory Peterson*

"Are there any birds around here that we can see?" a thin, middle-aged man asked Assistant Refuge Manager Dave Beall at the Bear River Migratory Bird Refuge Headquarters.

"Yes," Dave politely answered, "there are about 80 species on the refuge right now, mostly water birds."

Amazed by the man's question, I turned and rolled my eyes at Kit, who returned my glance with a stunned frown. The reason for our amazement was that it was physically impossible to have reached the refuge without driving across 15 miles of wetlands, which, though in private ownership, were teeming that day with ducks, shore birds, swallows, blackbirds, egrets and gulls. We had counted 22 species before we reached the refuge boundary. This man must have flown in by helicopter or

Great expanses of water, snow-capped mountains and families of geese are what Bear River Migratory Bird Refuge is all about.

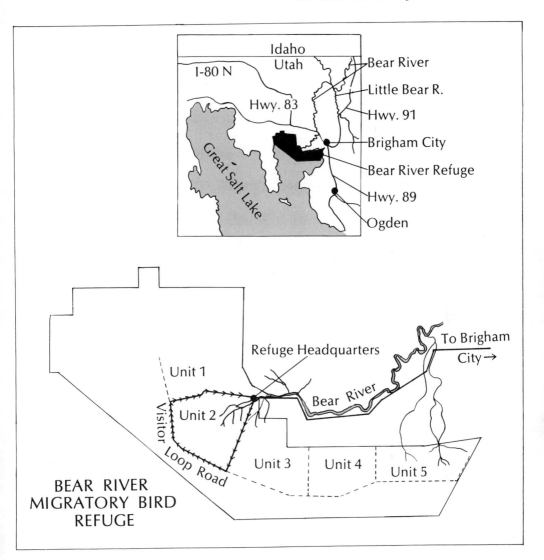

dropped in by parachute if he hadn't seen any birds between Brigham City and the headquarters building.

He had arrived, as we had, during late May, the best time of the year to see the greatest number of species at Bear River.

This area certainly was different from the canyon country of southeastern Arizona and the lush forest of Point Pelee, Ontario, where we had just visited. Bear River is almost totally treeless.

We were in the Upper Great Salt Lake Basin, surrounded on all sides by snow-capped mountains. Formed by the Wasatch Fault, Bear River Refuge, indeed all of the Great Salt Lake, is a remnant of a 20,000-square-mile inland sea called Lake Bonneville which existed 25,000 years ago.

The Bear River drainage system accounts for 80 percent of Great Salt Lake's water. It comes from the mountains, through the refuge and into Bear River Bay to the southwest and Willard Bay to the southeast. Both are reasonably fresh unless the wind has been blowing from the south. The flow of Bear River plus the restrictions of a railroad causeway and other dikes has limited the intrusion of salt water into Bear River Bay.

The tens of thousands of acres of shallow water found in and around Bear River Refuge are well suited to be one of America's prime waterfowl and shore bird breeding grounds. Mallards, gadwalls, blue-winged and cinnamon teal, northern shovelers, redheads and ruddy ducks all breed in Bear River Refuge, producing 20,000 ducklings a year. Gadwalls are the most abundant. American coots, not included in these figures, usually match the duck population. In addition, some 1,500 Canada geese are raised there each season. By fall, there are up to a half million waterfowl feeding in the refuge, including 16 species of ducks (200,000 pintails), 2 kinds of geese and whistling swans.

When the first explorers entered the Great Salt Lake Valley, they found it inhabited by Indians and wildlife. Captain Howard Stansbury gave the following description of what he saw at Bear River Bay in October, 1849:

> The marshes were covered by immense flocks of wild geese and ducks among which many swans were seen, being distinguishable by their size and the whiteness of their plumage. I had seen large flocks of these birds before, in various parts of our country, and especially upon the Potomac, but never did I behold anything like the immense numbers here congregated together. Thousands of acres, as far as the eye could reach, seemed literally covered with them, presenting a scene of busy, animated cheerfulness, in most graceful contrast with the dreary, silent solitude by which we were immediately surrounded.

One of the last great natural waterfowl factories left, Bear River Refuge accounts for 20,000 ducklings and 1,500 goslings each year.

A desire to preserve waterfowl made the refuge a reality in 1928, when Congress reacted to the urgings of duck-hunting interests in the northern Utah area.

The need to control avian botulism was another reason for establishing the Bear River Refuge. According to the best estimates, in 1910 alone a half million ducks perished near the mouth of Bear River from this toxin. Between 1,000 and 1,500 ducks still die annually from botulism, with a peak year in 1971 taking a toll of 50,000. Under the supervision of Dr. Wayne Jensen, the Fish and Wildlife Service is conducting research to find a control.

But ducks and geese are only a part of the attraction for bird watchers. An impressive list of shore birds, marsh birds and wading birds is reason enough to visit anytime between mid-March and the first snow.

One of the most interesting birds at Bear River was the western grebe. This pair went through the preliminaries to their spectacular courtship dance.

Black-necked stilts were among the common birds of Bear River's grassy wetlands. They were often seen with American avocets, long-billed curlews, willets and many species of waterfowl.

According to Dave Beall, the best time for waterfowl is late March and early April and again in late fall. For general viewing, the month of May is best. For nesting birds, the first two weeks in June are ideal. For sheer numbers, late summer is best. For shore, wading and marsh birds, it's the last two weeks in August.

We selected late May in order to combine the best general viewing period with the first nestings. We hit it right.

On the road from Brigham City, we came to a screeching stop just outside the city limits where the river had partly flooded the road. Sitting on cattails along the roadside were a half dozen yellow-headed blackbird males—all singing their croaky, gurgling calls. Though somewhat like the sound of a red-winged blackbird, the yellow-headed blackbird's song is far more startling.

Farther along the road, where a spillway flows under the highway, we stopped to identify swallows sitting on a barbed-wire fence. We discovered that we were looking at 5 different species: barn, tree, cliff, bank and rough-winged.

Nearby we had our first view of American avocets, black-necked stilts, long-billed curlews, willets and white-faced ibis, all of which are common breeders at Bear River.

Alkaline flats are numerous in the Bear River area. One such flat along the road was filled with California gulls and Forster's terns. It looked as though a convention of white birds was in session.

A few minutes later, we slammed on the brakes (we're hard on brakes) as 4 huge white pelicans glided over the road and landed in a large water area 100 yards away.

Not used to seeing so many cinnamon teal, we stopped often to watch mated pairs waddle into the cover of alkaline bulrush and salt grass.

By the time we reached the headquarters, we already felt at home at Bear River.

As we talked to Dave Beall in the office about the refuge, out of the corner of my eye I saw a family of Canada geese behind the building. A woman from Mesa, Arizona, was photographing the pair and their 5 goslings. Unable to resist, I left Kit talking with Dave about Bear River and joined the Arizona photographer outside. The goose family moved into the swift river current, traveled downstream a few yards and then waddled back on shore. There were several families of Canada geese with youngsters of varying ages around the headquarters building, but these particular goslings were very young, still having the fluffy yellow down of hatchlings. In a few weeks, as they begin to grow up, that pretty yellow ball of fluff will turn to drab gray.

Crossing a concrete bridge to the maintenance buildings, we watched swarms of cliff swallows build their adobe nests under the eaves. While one bird remained in the half-built cup, the other swallow gathered mud balls at the river's edge. Each cup had one bird in it waiting for its mate to bring more "mortar." Every time a flying swallow approached the housing development, each waiting bird turned its head to see if the arriving bird was its mate. The concert of head turning, accompanied by chipping and fluttering, was entertainment of high quality.

All visitors are directed to the 12-mile loop road that begins and ends at headquarters. The one-way gravel road circumscribes the dikes around the refuge's Unit 2. This is the only public road in the refuge. No trails exist, though plans call for the creation of at least one walking trail when funds become available.

Equipped with Bear River literature and an official bird list, we drove out the loop road. In less than a quarter of a mile, we stopped to listen to a strange rattling coming from the cattails—long-billed marsh wrens. Lots of them. Every few yards there was a singing male.

As we continued along the dike road, the water areas became extensive and ducks were more abundant. Here we found our first ruddy ducks. What a gaudy-looking fellow that male ruddy is, with his rusty-red back and sky-blue bill!

We found gadwalls and families of Canada geese very common.

Bear River is famous for its populations of breeding western grebes. I last saw one while traveling the West with my dad many years ago. What a thrill to drive up to a spillway where two pairs of western grebes were diving for food stirred up by

The loop road through Bear River is open to one-way traffic only . . . unless you are a privileged character.

A dapper drake ruddy performed for his hen along the loop road at Bear River.

In perfect concert, all eyes watched for a mate to bring the next ball of wet mud for cliff swallow nests in Bear River.

Heckle and Jeckle, two friendly ravens, watched as we ate lunch in the Bear River Refuge.

the tumbling water! We watched for thirty minutes, hoping to see the famous courtship dance in which both birds run across the water like two harnessed steeds pulling a chariot. The pairs did demonstrate the preliminaries to this ritual by rubbing their heads over their wings and tail feathers in a nervous preening action, but no runs were made.

Another very common bird was the ring-necked pheasant. It seemed we flushed a cockbird every few hundred yards along the dike roads.

At the first of two observation towers, we ate lunch. The cliff swallows building adobes under the tower entertained us, and we found some interesting songbirds in a row of small cottonwoods across the road. There were many yellow-headed blackbirds, but some smaller birds, too. A closer look turned up yellow-rumped (Audubon's), Wilson's and orange-crowned warblers and a rare find (not on the Bear River bird list), a northern waterthrush.

As we began to eat, a group from the Ogden Sierra Club drove up. As they watched the warblers, one member spotted a common loon on the water. A bit suspicious, we all glassed the loon, then happily added it to our list for the day.

Along the loop road we saw snowy egrets, great blue herons, California gulls, Forster's terns, pintails, blue-winged teal and mallards. We also added red-breasted mergansers, northern shovelers and redheads, as well as pied-billed grebes and American coots.

At the last bend before returning to headquarters, we spotted the woman photographer from Arizona taking pictures of American avocets. About 10 pairs were nesting on the mud flat. By standing very still, she was able to get close-ups of these dramatic-looking shore birds. I made a note to return to the spot later.

By the time we returned to headquarters, our bird list for the day had grown to 54.

After setting up our tent in the campground just outside the refuge gate, we headed toward Brigham City to try to find a burrowing owl reported to be about 4 miles away. En route, we passed two young men from Michigan who pointed out a snowy plover on the alkaline flats. The delicately marked white bird was another life lister for us.

Because burrowing owls dip every few seconds, the challenge for a photographer is to shoot between dips. Fresh disturbances on the mound were made by a gang of Brigham City motorcyclists.

On the road to the burrowing owl, we also added dowitchers, western sandpipers, marbled godwits and Wilson's phalaropes.

With our discovery of the burrowing owl nesting hole came an upsetting experience. We found four motorcyclists perched right on top of the mound in which the owl supposedly was nesting. As we approached, they ran up and down the mound, revving up their motors as they played with their cycles. At last, they tore off toward Brigham City in a cloud of dust and smoke. On close examination, we found the owl's burrow overrun with

A female California gull sat motionless on three eggs at the edge of the dike road at the Bear River National Wildlife Refuge.

California gulls nest in colonies along the Bear River roads.

This is not an ad for a 120mm-long cigarette. It is a long-billed curlew at the side of the road to the Bear River headquarters.

tire tracks, but not completely caved in. Not wanting to disturb the birds any further, we left immediately.

On our return from town, an owl was perched on top of the mound as if nothing had happened. By carefully and slowly driving into the road next to the bird, we got close enough to photograph it from the car. From a photographer's standpoint, burrowing owls are tricky. They bob every few seconds. You have to push the button between bobs.

We could see only one owl, which may have indicated that its mate was inside the burrow incubating or brooding young.

The temperature was around 75 degrees when we arrived on May 17. The next day was nearly perfect, with temperatures pushing toward 80 degrees. Little did we know what the weather gods had in store for us as we toured the refuge in summer clothes.

The first indications of a weather change occurred on the afternoon of the 18th when clouds formed in the west, but by sundown they had cleared off again. The radio report called for increased cloudiness on the 19th and rain by the 20th. Though the morning of the 19th was cloudy, we shot photos of long-billed curlews, eared grebes and California gulls. By noon it began to rain, and the radio weather forecast called for falling temperatures, high winds and heavy rain.

By the night of the 19th, the wind was up to a scary 30 mph as we huddled in our little tent. A more alarming forecast, including snow, drove us into the car for the night.

On the morning of May 20, we awakened to a light snow outside the car and heavy snows on the mountains surrounding Bear River Valley. The temperature was in the high 30s. The radio reported snow depths of up to 14 inches in nearby areas of northern Utah.

This experience, though somewhat exciting for us, should be fair warning to May visitors. It can get cold in Bear River Refuge, though temperatures usually rise to the 70s during the day.

The day after the storm, we went back to the mud flat

Following the late spring snowstorm with 30-mph winds, we dried our gear and resumed work at Bear River.

Bear River, where east meets west, was symbolized by this rare photograph of an eastern kingbird (bottom) and western kingbird as they shared a perch.

where the avocets were nesting. We found it partially flooded! The birds whose nests were in water had built them up with saltwort to keep the eggs out of the water. As we watched from a distance, the avocets worked furiously, gathering nesting material to keep ahead of the rising water. This was the first time I had witnessed this survival tactic, though I had read that black-necked stilts also do it.

Whether the storm brought them in or whether they had been there all the time we don't know, but thousands of swallows were huddled on the refuge roads. As we drove the loop, waves of barn, cliff, tree and rough-winged swallows rose ahead of our car and settled again as we passed.

Western kingbirds were common while we were at Bear River, but we didn't see an eastern kingbird until our fourth day. I took a very lucky photograph of the western and eastern kingbirds in the same bush. "East is east, and west is west" and Bear River is where they meet.

The storm brought in an invasion of western tanagers and lazuli buntings. They were almost as thick in Brigham as they were in the refuge.

"Pot licker" mallards visited our Bear River campsite every evening for a handout of wild bird seed.

There were also swarms of midges—nonbiting mosquito-like insects that live among the nettles and other plant life along the dikes. Sometimes they were so thick we could hardly see through the swarms.

We drove the loop many times that week and added new birds to the list on each trip. Caspian and black terns, Franklin's gulls, common ravens, spotted sandpipers, killdeers, American bitterns, black-billed magpies and yellow warblers were just a few.

As our week at Bear River neared an end, we had made friends with some of the local wildlife around headquarters. For example, there was the "pot licker" mallard couple who visited our tent site every night at suppertime. It became a ritual to have a little cup of grain ready for them as they waddled up from the marsh.

Then there was the "beep-beep" roadrunner-type chukar partridge who went speeding past the tent at what looked like 95 mph on his way to some unknown destination. Dave Beall told us that it was a survivor of a large release of chukars from a nearby hunting club. One time when we saw the bird, it was speeding down the road with a small boy in hot pursuit.

Our list for the week totaled 85. We were pleased with that number. Dave Beall had told us there were about 80 species on the refuge when we arrived.

We left Bear River with the impression that this refuge is one of the last places left in North America where one can see large numbers of water birds nesting, courting, raising young and completely at home in a well-preserved natural environment.

VISITOR TIPS

Recommended time to visit: Month of May. Also, late summer.

Clothing: We found temperatures to be in the 70s during the day and in the 50s at night, although we did get caught in a rare late-May snowstorm when the temperature dropped into the 30s, so plan your wardrobe accordingly. Have a good supply of insect repellent, especially if you are camping.

Lodging: Brigham City.

Restaurants: Brigham City.

Camping: A small camping area is provided outside the refuge gate. Also, Cache National Forest, 3 miles east of Brigham City, has camping facilities.

Picnic Areas: Picnic tables are provided in the camping area near the Visitor Center.

Reservations: In May you probably don't need them. In late summer, one or two weeks in advance. Write ahead for motel and camping information to:

> Bear River Migratory Bird Refuge
> P.O. Box 459
> Brigham City, Utah 84302
>
> Brigham City Chamber of Commerce
> Brigham City, Utah 84302

Rest Rooms: Only at the Visitor Center.

Telephone: Brigham City.

Gasoline: Brigham City.

Groceries: Brigham City has several supermarkets.

Hospital: Brigham City.

Airport: Salt Lake City.

Bird List: A checklist of 222 species of birds may be picked up at the Visitor Center.

7

Coast of Maine:

Down East Islands

> *When I think of Maine I think first of the rock coast, the islands and the sea. The hundreds of islands are but remnants of mainland hills, now isolated by the encircling sea, standing offshore, their rocks bared to the erosive action of the surf and the tides. The most seaward of these marooned hilltops, bereft of trees and barely clearing the waves, are the homes of thousands of birds of the littoral who find in these oceanic tenements their key to survival.*
>
> —Roger Tory Peterson

Of all the places to find birds along the Maine coast, perhaps the best for a variety of species is Mount Desert Island (Acadia National Park). Some ornithologists have referred to Mount Desert (pronounced de-zert) as the "warbler capital of the United States," for the island is home to at least 21 species of breeding wood warblers.

But one must be aware that birding here is a totally different challenge from birding in other places covered in this book. It is necessary to be a bird *listener* as well as a bird *watcher* to recognize and fully appreciate the birds of Mount Desert Island.

When you're trying to identify northern wood warblers and other Canadian Life Zone birds, it is sometimes impossible to

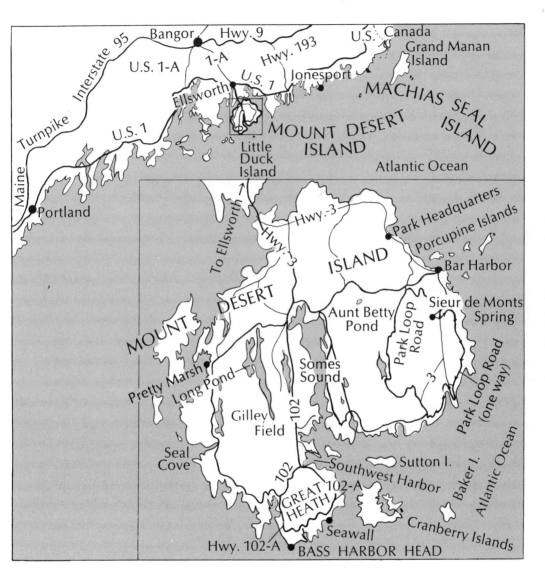

actually see the birds you hear. Knowing the songs of each makes identification easier and much more enjoyable.

When Roger Peterson and I were creating the final list of our twelve hot spots, the inclusion of the coast of Maine delighted me because I knew this meant a return to my beloved "mystic isle of Mount Desert."

Kit and I arrived on the island on June 15, the peak of the bird breeding season. With the help of Ralph "Bud" Long, Jr., and his wife, Pat, we made plans for at least a week of fieldwork.

I met Bud in 1949 when we were boys exploring the island for birds and ocean life. In the intervening years, Bud has become a recognized and highly respected ornithologist. He has been a great help to James Bond, a summer resident on Mount Desert and author of the definitive guide *Native Birds of Mount Desert Island.* Bond is also author of *Birds of the West Indies.*

The island is divided into two distinct birding areas: southwestern Mount Desert, where the Canadian species are found, and northeastern Mount Desert, where more southern birds predominate. These divisions are separated by Somes Sound, the only true fjord in North America.

The reason for southern birdlife in the northeastern section is that in 1947 a devastating fire leveled 17,000 acres of mature forest, creating habitat more suitable for field and meadow birds, which then extended their ranges.

By far the more interesting of the two sections, from our point of view, was the southwestern corner, where the forests and wetlands look as though they have been there since the last Ice Age. The extreme southern tip is a mecca for warbler watchers.

Just after daylight on the morning of June 16, Kit, Bud and I found ourselves sloshing into Great Heath, one of the three or four birding hot spots in the southwestern area. Less than a mile west of the Seawall Campground on the north side of the road, Great Heath is *the* spot for breeding palm warblers, Lincoln sparrows and yellow-bellied flycatchers.

Water in most of the Heath is never too deep to walk through even during the rainy season. The 16th of June was one of those typical Maine days . . . wet, foggy and somewhat cool. The path into the Heath was about as wet as Bud could recall. Nevertheless, rubber boots kept us dry.

Emerging from the deep woodland path into the open bog was like entering an inner sanctum. The Heath is nearly a half mile across and is surrounded by black spruce. Most of the spruce and shrubs growing inside are less than 10 feet high, having been stunted by water and lingering ice.

Standing on a floating carpet of mosses and lichen, George and Kit Harrison watched a Lincoln sparrow in the boughs of a black spruce.

Walking across the Heath was like walking across a mattress. Underfoot were sphagnum moss, reindeer lichen and a great variety of bog plants such as arethusa, Labrador tea, baked appleberry, bog rosemary, chokeberry and pitcher plants. Even in the driest spots, the Heath seems to be a floating mass of plant life. My standing camera tripod moved if anyone walked within 10 or 15 feet of it.

The foggy, damp and cool weather muffled the sounds of singing birds, but all the common summer birds were there. Most of the palm warblers (early nesters) were feeding young, and only a few males were singing. Earlier in the spring, dozens of palms sing in that same spot.

The Lincoln sparrows, discovered nesting there only a few years ago by Bud and a friend, were broadcasting their purple finch–like songs from the boughs of stunted black spruce trees.

Yellow-bellied flycatchers sounded off with their "til-lic,"

A palm warbler, one of the 19 species of warblers we saw at Mount Desert Island, watched as we searched for its nest.

as other Heath residents chimed in. Nashville and black-throated green warblers, yellowthroats, purple finches, red-breasted nuthatches, ruby-crowned kinglets, winter wrens and white-throated sparrows were a few of those we heard and saw.

Across the road and a little to the west are the Wonderland Trail and parking lot. After dragging our boots around the Heath for a couple of hours, we welcomed the change to hiking shoes and a well-defined trail.

One of Mount Desert's best birding trails is Wonderland. Here we added to our list several more warblers, including a blackpoll near the site where Bud Long had found the first blackpoll nest one year earlier.

Here our warbler scenario continued: redstarts, black-throated greens, parulas, black-and-whites, magnolias, yellow-rumps (myrtles) and blackpolls. At one point early on the trail we heard four black-throated greens sound off in order, as if answering to the First Sergeant's roll call. The population density of black-throated greens must have been as high there as anywhere in the world.

The sound of the blackpoll warbler's high-pitched trill was one of the highlights of the day. Bud found the first nest on the island in June, 1974, at this same spot near the end of the trail where the spruce meets the ocean.

The amazing thing about Wonderland is its contrast to the Great Heath just across the road. Wonderland is dry and rocky, with a lush understory of bunchberry, bayberry and heather. The trail is edged by beautiful white birch and red spruce, which merge into pitch pine near the ocean and then back to red spruce at the edge of the sea.

On one side you hear warblers and kinglets singing. Turning to the ocean side you see eider ducks, black guillemots and herring gulls bobbing in the water just offshore. This is the joy of the coast of Maine . . . where spruce meets the sea and where warblers and water birds are neighbors.

Back in the car, we moved west another mile, past Ship Harbor to the third hot spot on the southwest tip—Bass Harbor Head. Driving down the road to the lighthouse, we parked in the U.S. Coast Guard parking lot and walked back along the road on which we had driven in. Here lies the prettiest of all the spruce forests on Mount Desert Island. We explored both sides of the road, where tall white spruce and balsam firs give a cathedral-like feeling to the moss-carpeted area below.

It was still misting, and we were reminded of how close we were to the ocean by puffs of fog rolling past lichen-covered trees. The rich damp smell of sphagnum mixed with the salty sea breeze. The scene was further enhanced by the accompaniment of the Bass Harbor bell that tolled every few seconds. Were we birding in London? Not according to the kinds of birds we heard all around us, such as the bay-breasted warbler overhead. This road is one of the few places on Mount Desert where bay-breasteds can be found readily. Blackburnians, yellow-

Along the road to Bass Harbor Head, we explored the prettiest of all spruce forests on Mount Desert Island. There we added the bay-breasted, Blackburnian and parula warblers to our growing list.

rumps (myrtles), black-throated greens, parulas (singing both songs), magnolias, yellowthroats, Nashvilles and redstarts brought our warbler total for the day to 12. We also heard both kinglets sing. For some reason, it's particularly hard for me to remember which of the two kinglet songs is which, although they have distinctly different sounds. Maybe it is because the bold golden-crowned has a meek high-pitched squeak, while the timid ruby-crowned has a jumbled, rollicking, loud chorus with many variations. We also heard brown creepers, winter wrens, red-breasted nuthatches, purple finches, hermit thrushes and juncos.

Before leaving Bass Harbor Head, Bud tried to "squeak up" some birds next to the lighthouse. By kissing the back of his hand or knuckle, he created a squeaking noise that sounded like a baby bird. It really worked. Immediately, we had a parula, a redstart and a yellowthroat in front of us—all nervous and chipping in response to Bud's squeak.

The morning was about over, but we drove back to our camp at Southwest Harbor by way of Gilley Field, a few miles northwest of the village. Bud felt certain we would find a black-throated blue warbler along the National Park road leading into the area. Sure enough, on our second stop, near a stand of small spruce trees, the "zer-zer-zwee" reverberated through the woods. It was the first black-throated blue I'd heard in years. We added a Canada warbler and an ovenbird to our list, which brought our warbler total for that morning to 15.

When the weather cleared, we explored other parts of Acadia National Park and the island. We discovered that there are only a couple of National Park picnic grounds on the island and that Pretty Marsh is the best. In fact, it is the most beautiful picnic ground I've ever seen. Located in a deep spruce-and-cedar forest bordering Pretty Marsh Harbor, the area is parklike in appearance and cathedral-like in atmosphere. Not many birds were singing at noon, but we did hear black-throated greens, Blackburnians, winter wrens, red-breasted nuthatches and black-capped chickadees. Along the shore, at low tide, clamming is excellent. We watched a father and his several sons in less than an hour dig a couple of hundred clams on the stony beach.

We would have been happy to spend all of our time in the deeply wooded area of the southwest corner of the island, but for variety's sake one day we drove to the other side of Mount Desert, where Bar Harbor and Park Headquarters are located. Here we found the more southern species as we ate lunch at Sieur de Monts Spring. Just as the books said, there were many non-Canadian types, including a veery, a red-eyed vireo and a downy woodpecker, plus an ovenbird and yellow and chestnut-sided warblers, which brought our warbler total to 17.

Other excellent birding spots on Mount Desert Island are Aunt Betty Pond, Lurvey Spring and Long Hill (south of Southwest Harbor just beyond the point where Highways 102 and 102A split for the first time). It was at Long Hill that we found Wilson's warblers and boreal chickadees in profusion. The Wilson's was warbler number 18.

We found warbler number 19, the northern waterthrush, west of Seal Cove Pond, on the west side of the island. We also found a pair of red crossbills behaving as if they were nesting. A red crossbill nest has never been found on Mount Desert.

Birding is only one of many interesting things to do on Mount Desert Island. In fact, it isn't possible to write a chapter on Mount Desert without some mention of lobsters and clams. Certainly part of the pleasure of being on the coast of Maine is the availability of Maine seafood. Lobster, of course, is king. Kit and I made it an unwritten rule to eat some kind of fresh seafood at every evening meal while in Maine—and lobster at least every other night. In addition to the freshness of the seafood, it cost 30 to 60 percent less than the same fish in the city marketplaces.

It seemed to us that camping and clambakes went together. Our L. L. Bean lobster/clam steamer, filled with shellfish and covered with seaweed, provided a repast fit for any king.

Bud and Pat hold their own nightly clambake for the public and prepare it in the traditional Down East fashion over an open fire. Offered complete with corn on the cob and fresh blueberry cake, the lobsters and clams they prepare are the finest anywhere.

There were a few more birds we wanted to find before leaving Mount Desert. Bud told us that the sharp-tailed sparrows nest in Bass Harbor Marsh. One sunny afternoon late in the week, we stopped the car along Route 102 just before crossing the bridge. We walked into the marsh on the right side of the road (as you face the mountains). As we made our way along the grassy flat, the water got deeper, but we were urged on by what sounded like Bud's description of a sharptail's song just ahead of us. As we picked our way from dry hammock to dry hammock, we flushed a very nondescript sparrow that flew like a youngster. According to the field guides, the adult sharptails have a weak, short flight on their breeding grounds. Had we seen one?

We pressed on and flushed two more, one of which flew to the edge of the marsh, sat in a bush and sang the strangest sparrow song I've heard. It was my first sharp-tailed sparrow. The song was more like a short hissing sound—like steam being released—followed by two chips. Peterson described it with the chips preceding the "psh-h-h-h-h-h." Regardless, it was a strange-sounding sparrow.

A DAY AT DUCK ISLAND

The reason for my first visit to Mount Desert Island in 1949 was to help with the filming of my father's movie *The Mystic Isle of Mount Desert,* an adventure film he presented in schools and at service-club meetings during his many years as a platform speaker.

A part of that film was a visit to Little Duck, a small oceanic island 7 miles off Mount Desert. Five men and boys spent a wonderful week there camping and exploring the bird and sea life of the island. In addition to Bud Long and me, there were our fathers and Bud's younger brother, Benny. Our week on Little Duck was memorable.

It seemed appropriate, therefore, that a part of this chapter on the Maine coast should be a revisit to Little Duck Island. Bud was instrumental in including Kit and me on a daylong field trip to Little Duck with the Philadelphia Academy of Natural Science.

As our high-speed boats skipped across the swells between

Turning our backs on Mount Desert Island, we sped to another adventure on Little Duck Island, 7 miles out to sea.

Great black-backed and herring gulls are among Little Duck's first-class citizens. This welcoming committee watched carefully as we made our way through their nesting grounds.

Mount Desert and Little Duck, I tried to remember some of the details of that same trip twenty-six years earlier. So much had happened to the rest of the world since then, and I wondered if Little Duck had changed too.

It took only twenty minutes to make the run over open sea that had required an hour or more in 1949. (No public service to

Bud reached down a Leach's storm-petrel burrow and came out with an adult bird that had been incubating its one egg.

Little Duck is available. You must hire a lobsterman or private boat owner to take you.) As our boats neared the shoreline, great black-backed and herring gulls rose in masses off the rocks and circled in great waves. I noticed that double-crested cormorants were present in large numbers. They had not been there in 1949.

Climbing the steep hill to the grassy meadows, Bud was the first to discover a Leach's storm-petrel burrow. Reaching into

During the incubation period, petrels will emerge from the burrow only at night to trade places with the mate that has spent the day at sea.

Petrels are members of the tube-nosed family of birds, which includes other pelagic species such as albatrosses, fulmars and shearwaters. We knew when we were near a petrel burrow at Little Duck by the musky odor we detected.

the hole all the way to his shoulder, he pulled out an adult petrel that had been incubating a single egg at the end of the burrow.

Bud spread its tail feathers to show our group its best field mark, a white triangle at the base of its tail. Otherwise, the bird was a nondescript sooty gray. The tube on top of its bill distinguished it as a member of the tube-nosed bird family, which also includes other seabirds such as albatrosses, fulmars, shearwaters and other petrels. All are pelagic birds, spending the majority of their lives at sea. Petrels are nocturnal birds and during the incubation period will trade places with their mates in the burrows each night before daylight.

Bud told the group that he could smell the petrels even before he found the burrow. Sure enough, we too could smell the musky odor.

After everyone had a good look, Bud released the bird in its burrow and we moved to the gull fields.

The great black-backed gulls were feeding youngsters. Some of the chicks were more than half grown and were found crouching silently in the high grass. A few blackbacks still had eggs, as did most herring gulls.

Kit found two herring gull nests with eggs beginning to hatch. When we held the pipping eggs to our ears, we could hear the chicks inside pecking at the shell and calling faint little peeps.

The cormorant colony was of great interest. The birds had nested only a foot or two apart, and most nests contained gangly black youngsters, all shaking and weaving their necks around and begging for food even from us.

The visit to the cormorant colony was a lesson in survival. Dead chicks were scattered throughout the nesting area, having either fallen out of the nest or been killed by gulls.

Moving on down the rocky shore, we flushed several black guillemots from their nesting sites under rocks. Kit was particularly good at hearing the guillemots stirring under the rocks before they flew. We tried several times, without success, to photograph one, but they always flew out another exit. These pigeon-sized birds had jet-black, feltlike bodies with large white wing patches and red feet. Their two brown-blotched cream-colored eggs were laid on bare rocks and pebbles.

Kit found a great black-backed gull youngster in the high grass of Little Duck. Almost as large as its parents, it was still unable to fly or feed itself.

A baby herring gull is about to make its debut at Little Duck Island. Kit found several gull eggs "pipping."

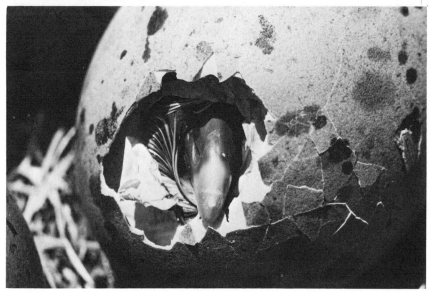

With members of the Philadelphia Academy of Natural Science, we toured the cormorant colony on Little Duck Island.

Eider ducklings were everywhere. The larger ones swam in flotillas, while the smaller ones were running around quacking in raspberry patches. Several people from the Philadelphia Academy were shocked when a black-backed gull seized an eider duckling and carried it off for dinner.

A spruce woodland on the crown of Little Duck is inhabited by an interesting variety of warblers. We heard magnolias and redstarts as we walked through the interior, and yellow warblers and yellowthroats around the edges. In 1949 our group had discovered a blackpoll warbler nesting in that woods, but the blackpoll was not heard as we made our way through this beautiful primeval woodland.

Gangly and homely, these young double-crested cormorants begged for food from the human intruders on Little Duck Island.

Just off the shore of Little Duck, two black guillemots watched as we made our way past their nest hidden under the rocks.

Little Duck Island has a good population of eider ducks. On the day we were there, little eiders seemed to be everywhere in the grass and among the rocks along the shore.

Little Duck looked the same as I recalled it twenty-six years earlier. The settlement of the cormorant colony was the only noticeable change. Otherwise, the island matched my memory of gulls, guillemots, eiders and warblers . . . and all seemed to be thriving.

The credit for keeping Little Duck as it always was should go to the National Audubon Society, which acquired it as a bird sanctuary in 1934. The island is an excellent example of what can and should be done all along our coasts. The preservation of key island habitat is essential to the health of our delicate seabird populations. So many islands that were once like Little Duck have already been developed and exploited to suit man's needs—or at least what he thinks are his needs.

MACHIAS SEAL ISLAND

There is another tiny island, about 25 acres in size, that lies between Maine (U.S.A.) and New Brunswick (Canada), half in the Bay of Fundy (Canada) and half in the Gulf of Maine (U.S.A.). It is Machias Seal, or Seal, Island.

Though the Canadians and the Americans cannot agree on who owns it, they do agree that Machias is a fabulous oceanic-bird island that requires protection and careful management.

Since I was a small boy paging through bird books, I've known about Machias Seal Island . . . the home of the common puffin.

As our boat dropped anchor a few hundred feet off the rocky shore of Machias Seal on June 21, flocks of puffins flushed from nearby rocks, circled around the shoreline and passed between us and the dory coming to pick us up. The island was alive with seabirds—arctic terns, razorbills, common murres and, of course, puffins. I had chills. This was no fantasy; I was really there.

During the two-hour boat trip from Jonesport we passed the time with stories and descriptions of the birds of Seal Island. Our captain, Barna Norton, had arranged to have us on board with Jack Russell, the well-known Canadian lighthouse keeper on Machias for ten years, from 1965 to 1974. He was

As if guarding Machias Seal Island, an arctic tern stations itself only 3 feet from its nest and two eggs.

returning to his beloved island after nearly a year's absence. Jack's son, Malcolm, who had grown up on Seal Island and was now Assistant Lighthouse Keeper there, was on board too. Jack's wife was also along for this trip home to Machias Seal.

At close range, I was surprised at how small the island looked. The high ground where the three buildings and lighthouse are located is a grassy area only about 1,000 feet long and 300 feet wide. The rocks surround the grass down to the water.

Stanley Green, the new lighthouse keeper, loaded Jack, Kit and me into his dory for the first trip ashore. As we walked up the path to the buildings, I noticed an arctic tern sitting on a sign that said "Bird Sanctuary."

When Jack Russell first became lighthouse keeper in 1965, he found only about 2,000 puffins on the island. That number has now doubled. In fact, all the seabirds have increased except

Since I was a small boy I've known about Machias Seal Island, the home of the common puffin. This was the moment a dream became a reality.

Both arctic terns (pictured) and common terns nested in abundance on Machias Seal. In fact, it was difficult to keep from being dive-bombed by the terns as we walked past their nests.

From our blind at Machias Seal we photographed razorbills (like the one pictured) and puffins as they landed a few feet away and then disappeared under the rocks to care for eggs and young.

This little arctic tern will fly from Machias Seal Island to somewhere south of the equator on the longest migration flight of any species.

The bird in the middle with the thin bill is a common murre. All the others are razorbills. Both were among the common seabirds we saw on Machias Seal.

terns, which reportedly suffered recently from a premature burning of the island's weeds. "There were ten times that many here last year," Russell insisted, "but the rest of the island is exactly the way we left it."

Barna Norton's boat, *Chief*, makes almost daily trips to Machias Seal. Kit and I were the 69th and 70th visitors for the year. The year before there was a total of 850 visitors to the island.

Recalling what tourists can do to places such as Kenya, Baja and the Galápagos, I asked Malcolm if he thought visitors were hurting the island.

"So far nothing has been destroyed, nothing hurt," Malcolm responded.

Norton's boat stays at the island for only three hours, so Kit and I were eager to start shooting pictures. To get to either of the two photo blinds, we had to walk across a grassy area between the buildings and the rocks. We quickly discovered that this grassy area is controlled by the arctic terns. Anyone who enters it does so at his own risk. And risk it was! As soon as we started across the path the dive-bombing attacks began. At least a dozen terns swooped down on us, striking the tops of our heads with their sharp bills and even splattering us with their foul-smelling droppings. We quickly learned to protect ourselves by waving a hand over our heads. The reason for these attacks was obvious. Sets of two blotched olive-colored eggs were spotted in the grass every few feet. We stepped over three nests right on the path!

Bloody but unbowed, we breathlessly entered the protection of the blind. Within minutes, we had terns, razorbills and puffins landing on the rocks just outside the blind. Photos were easy and fun to take.

Unlike terns, both razorbills and puffins hide their single eggs under rocks. Though most puffin eggs hatch after July 1, a few adults were already carrying fish in their bills, indicating that some chicks had already hatched.

Jack Russell explained that his son Malcolm had discovered how a puffin can catch four to six fish at one time. "Straight teeth located on its tongue push the fish to the roof of the mouth, where another set of fishhook teeth holds it secure while the bird gathers more fish. It swims into a school of small fish, snags one, turns around and makes another run, which explains why you see fish heads and tails coming out of both sides of the bill," Jack concluded.

During his tenure at Machias Seal, Jack learned a great deal about puffins. He related how the young are deserted by the adults when they are ready to fend for themselves. The youngsters parade in long lines around the island at night in a madcap binge, jumping off rocks and playing follow-the-leader for three days until hunger drives them into the sea. There they learn to fish on their own, and they do not return to the island until they mature two years later.

After more than an hour in the blind, Kit and I risked our clean jackets again by crossing the tern colony, stopping long enough at one nest to photograph a newly hatched chick. Though only a few hours old, the chick, guided by instinct, crouched and remained motionless while we were present.

A warden of the Canadian Wildlife Service, Richard Blacquere, was helpful in showing us a puffin in a crevice sitting on its one egg. I could just barely see the colorful bill between the rocks.

Blacquere also pointed out a common murre sitting on a rock among several razorbills. Both are black and white and about the same size, but they have distinctly different bills. The murre's was thin and pointed, while the razorbill's was fat and wedge-shaped like the puffin's.

In a little over three hours, we recorded 21 species of birds on Machias Seal, including some surprises such as an indigo bunting, a yellow warbler, a hermit thrush, a Traill's flycatcher, a tree swallow (no trees), a barn swallow (building a nest *inside* one of the photo blinds) and three laughing gulls. A Sabine gull had been sighted there earlier that week.

Our time on Machias was so short we could hardly believe it was over. In retrospect, it was one of the most exciting times we had experienced in visiting our hot spots.

It was a great relief to see this famous hot spot doing so well. The preservation of this seabird colony is unquestionably a tribute to the cooperative efforts of both countries. But like Little Duck, Machias Seal is a fragile ecosystem requiring careful management and protection against man's insatiable appetite for more land.

VISITOR TIPS

Recommended time to visit: June.

Clothing: Maine weather is unpredictable, so pack rain gear. A couple of the days we were on Mount Desert were really hot, but most of the time we were comfortable wearing a sweater or light jacket. Hiking shoes or boots are a good idea, especially if you plan to tackle some of the mountain paths.

Lodging: Stop at the Visitor Center on Thompson Island as you drive onto Mount Desert. You can find out there what's available, where and the approximate cost. We suggest you make Mount Desert your base of operations for your birding on the coast of Maine, as we did. Little Duck Island is just a few miles off its shore, and Jonesport, where the boat leaves for Machias Seal Island, is less than an hour-and-a-half drive.

Restaurants: Southwest Harbor, Bar Harbor and Seawall have wonderful restaurants. Or, try a Down East clambake with Bud and Pat Long!

Camping: Acadia National Park has two campgrounds, one at Seawall and the other at Black Woods. Also, there are numerous private campgrounds outside the park.

Picnic Areas: There are five on Mount Desert: Hadley Point, Thompson Island, Seawall, Bear Brook (on the park loop road just beyond Sieur de Monts Spring) and, our favorite, Pretty Marsh. No picnic facilities are provided on either Little Duck or Machias Seal, but if you take your trash with you when you leave the islands, you may take a lunch.

Reservations: Make reservations about two weeks in advance. Write ahead for motel and camping information to:

> Acadia National Park Headquarters
> Hulls Cove, Maine 04644
> (207) 288-3338

Thompson Island Information Service
Route 3 at the Bridge
Mount Desert Island, Maine 04660

Rest Rooms: On Mount Desert they are at Sieur de Monts Spring and at all the picnic areas. Machias Seal has an outhouse, but there are none on Little Duck Island.

Telephone: Public phones can be found in nearly all of the towns on Mount Desert.

Gasoline: Gas stations can be found in almost all of the towns and along the roads between towns.

Groceries: Small markets are located in almost all of the little towns on Mount Desert. We also made daily visits to the wharves in either Southwest Harbor or Bernard for fresh seafood.

Hospital: Bar Harbor has a hospital. Southwest Harbor and Northeast Harbor both have medical centers.

Airport: It is possible to fly to the Bar Harbor airport on commercial airlines, but the nearest big airport is in Bangor.

Bird List: We picked up a list of 314 birds from the Acadia National Park Visitor Center, but it was bulky and hard to work with. If you find a copy of James Bond's booklet *Native Birds of Mount Desert*, buy it. Bond tells where the species of Mount Desert's birds are likely to be found.

8

Gaspé:

Seabird Bastion

I believe the gannet ledges of Bonaventure to be one of the greatest ornithological spectacles of the continent, more impressive even than the populous murre and auk colonies farther north. The size and whiteness of the gannets give them a visual impact lacking in lesser fowl.

—*Roger Tory Peterson*

Near the tip of the Gaspé Peninsula in Quebec lies a little village called Percé. Like all villages on the peninsula, Percé is quaint, a bit primitive and very French. But from a birder's standpoint, it is quite different from any of the other villages. It is the jumping-off point for Bonaventure Island, the world's largest gannetry and one of the most spectacular seabird colonies found anywhere.

Only 2 miles from Percé in the Gulf of St. Lawrence, Bonaventure Island is easily reached by boats that ferry visitors to and from the island several times a day. Most of the people who

One of the greatest sights in all the bird world can be seen from a boat passing the 250-foot-high nesting cliffs of Bonaventure Island.

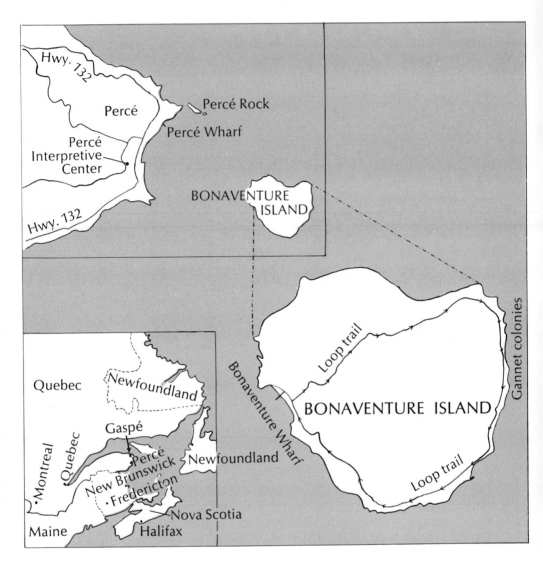

go there go just to see the hundreds of thousands of gannets, razorbills, common murres, black guillemots, black-legged kittiwakes and common puffins that nest on the cliffs from May through August.

Discovered by Jacques Cartier during his first exploration

Only 2 miles from the Percé wharf in the Gulf of St. Lawrence, Bonaventure Island is easily reached by boat. The nesting cliffs are on the far side of the circular island.

of the New World in 1534, Bonaventure Island has suffered for four hundred years from human habitation and exploitation. When Europeans first came to North America, seabird colonies were a blessing to sailors, who used them as fresh meat. Later, fishermen looked to the birds as a source of bait and eggs. When these early fishermen arrived on the island in May, they usually found partially incubated eggs, which were unpalatable. So they smashed them—to stimulate the laying of fresh eggs, which they would then collect.

By the early 1900s, the Bonaventure bird colonies were declining, but it was not until 1919 that the eastern and northern cliffs of the island were declared a federal migratory-bird sanctuary. In 1972, the entire island was made a provincial park and all residents had to leave.

Kit and I arrived in Percé on June 24, following our coast-of-Maine adventure. The trip through New Brunswick and along the southern shore of the Gaspé Peninsula was most pleasant except for the condition of the Quebec highways. The pavement was full of chuckholes and very irregular, requiring speeds of less than 45 mph to keep from damaging our car. We appreciated U.S. highways more after that drive.

Our first stop was at the Percé Wildlife Centre, one of only five Canadian Wildlife Service interpretive centers in all of Canada. Réal Bisson, the officer in charge, briefed us on Bonaventure Island and the bird life of the Percé area. He gave us several pamphlets, including an official checklist for the birds of the Percé area.

He explained that there are a half dozen seabird species on Bonaventure, but that the gannets are the best known and of greatest concern. The 18,000 pairs on the island make Bonaventure the largest of the six gannetries in North America.

Bisson also explained that the gannets can be seen in two ways: by landing and walking across the top of the island to the ocean cliffs or by circling the island in a boat for a full view of the nesting cliffs from below. Kit and I would do both.

Following our talk with Bisson, we took a tour of the new interpretive center to find out more about the seabirds and local sea life, as well as about the cod, lobster and other marine industries of the area. We discovered that birding just outside the center was excellent and added a pine grosbeak to our master bird list for the year.

Percé is blessed with two beautiful provincial park camping areas, one for tents only and one for RV campers only. The tent area, where we camped, is an easy walk of about three blocks to the town wharf where the ferryboats leave for the island.

We rose early on June 25 in order to board the first boat for Bonaventure. It was the 7:30 workers' boat, which goes directly to the island dock rather than circling the island as the tourist boats do. Bisson had told us that the trick for photographers is to get to the far side of the island as early as possible for the best eastern light. In June, the sun rises in Quebec at about 4:30 A.M., and by 8:30 it is already high in the sky. He had said that by the time you cross the 2 miles of open sea between Percé and Bonaventure, climb the road to the top of the island and then walk down the other side to the gannet colony (about 1¾ miles), another hour has been consumed.

From the meadows of Bonaventure Island we looked back on Percé Rock and the village of Percé. Our adventure with the gannets was about to begin.

It was doubly hard for us to rush across the wooded island to the gannetry because birding along the trail was very good.

Bonaventure Island is an almost perfect circle, 2 miles across at any location. The highest elevation is 450 feet, and the cliffs on the northeast side, where most of the seabirds nest, rise abruptly to a height of 250 feet above the sea.

The trail from the dock to the top of the island is a bit steep, but not too strenuous. It begins in open grassy fields which slope sharply from the sea, affording a breathtaking view back to Percé Rock and the village of Percé. Then the trail enters a balsam fir and spruce forest which in the nesting season abounds with Tennessee, black-throated green and magnolia warblers, pine siskins, purple finches, hermit thrushes and fox sparrows.

We were surprised to find that Tennessee warblers were among the most common songbirds on Bonaventure. We had searched for them for days on Mount Desert Island without success.

Another surprise was the number of singing fox sparrows along the way. I had never been on fox sparrow breeding grounds before and did not recognize the song at first.

We knew when we were getting close to the gannet colony by the odor we detected as we left the woods and started downhill into open fields. It was decidedly a fishy smell, coming from the droppings of hundreds of thousands of seabirds.

The sight of the first gannet sailing overhead was exciting. Its graceful flight on long, narrow, tapered wings reminded me of the boobies I had seen in the Galápagos. The northern gannet is the only member of that family which nests in the north.

A few hundred yards farther on we looked onto one of the most spectacular birding sights of my life. Just ahead of us green grass ended and a carpet of snow-white gannets began. As if someone had been there ahead of us and lined them up on the edge of the cliff, the gannets were all facing in the same direction, side by side, only inches apart. Until 1974, visitors could walk right up to the birds; now a rail fence keeps everyone about 30 feet from the nearest nests. But even from behind the fence, my telephoto lenses allowed me to photograph the intimate behavior of gannet life.

It was immediately obvious that gannets are very affectionate creatures. The colony had both eggs and small chicks on June 25, but courtship displays were still common. We watched bird after bird bring gifts of seaweed to its mate, who tucked the offerings into the nest, sometimes around a downy chick.

Each time a mate returned to the colony, the two birds greeted each other with much chatter and neck rubbing. They caressed each other with bills, necks, heads and even wings. Often they pointed their necks high into the air and then entwined necks and heads in a display of touching and rubbing.

To fly away from the colony, a bird had to flop its way to the edge of the cliff, and by half falling, half beating its wings on the ground, it managed to become airborne. The least hazardous route to the take-off gully at the edge of the cliff was around the colony on the green grass. Any route through the colony was fraught with pecking, wing beating and squawking. The sounds of the gannets reminded us of a turkey farm filled with a thousand gobblers.

We were engrossed for hours in the behavioral activity in the gannet colony. For example, we noticed that each bird knew exactly where its nest was and, without hesitation, folded its wings and dropped into the white mass at precisely the right spot.

Gannets are very fussy birds, frequently arranging and rearranging nesting material. Sometimes they stole twigs from a neighbor's nest only a foot away.

We could easily distinguish the first-year breeders. They were at the outer edge of the colony and had some remnant black flecks of immature plumage on their wings.

One such pair had just selected a nesting site (at this late date!) on the extreme outer edge. To establish ownership of their little plot of ground about 2 feet by 2 feet, they engaged in continual sparring matches with the nesting pairs closest to them. Locking bills, they would fume and fuss, pull and peck, only to go back to gentle nuzzling with their mates.

Pairs will often occupy the nesting site from the year before, unless seniority allows them to move into the inner circle and onto the prime ledges.

A single egg is laid in a moss-lined, bowl-shaped hollow

We watched gannets at Bonaventure plunge into the sea from up to 400 feet. Air-filled cells around their necks and shoulders cushioned the impact.

The 18,000 pairs of gannets on the island make Bonaventure the largest of the six gannetries in North America.

Until just recently, visitors could walk right into the gannet colony at Bonaventure. Now a fence keeps people from disturbing the nesting birds.

Each time a bird returned to the gannet colony on Bonaventure, mates would greet each other with much caressing of bills, necks, heads and even wings.

Gannets are very fussy birds, frequently arranging and rearranging the nesting materials while they incubate their single egg.

built on top of a pile of debris. By mid-June most of the eggs are laid, and by late June the first naked chicks appear.

Gannets are very attentive parents, though their feeding habits look primitive. Kit and I watched the rather repulsive feeding performance as an adult opened its beak and the youngster plunged its tiny head inside to eat regurgitated partially digested fish.

Like boobies, gannets have a remarkable method of fishing. With the aid of their binocular vision (both eyes in front), they locate food from surprising heights. Then, from as high as 400 feet, they plunge to the water with such force that the water splashes up to 10 feet. These dives are cushioned by air-filled cells beneath the skin around the bird's neck and shoulders and connected to the lungs. Its elastic throat allows the passage of fish weighing as much as four pounds.

By September the young are ready to fend for themselves. After days of hesitation, the fledglings will hurl themselves over the cliff to the water 200 feet below. Some die on the rocks in their first attempt at flight, but most land in the water, not to return to these cliffs until they have matured to breeding age four or five years later.

During their juvenile years, they spend their summers far out at sea and their winters with the adults off the coasts of the southern United States, Cuba and Mexico. When they have matured, they return to Bonaventure Island with the other adults in April, when the snow still remains on the cliffs. They are believed to mate for life.

A climbing sun forced us to move along the fence and down the east side of the island. We again entered a fir/spruce woods filled with warblers. Blackpolls, bay-breasteds, black-and-whites, black-throated greens, Tennessees, northern parulas, magnolias, winter wrens and kinglets were common.

The ocean and cliffs again came into sight at a place called Lazy Beach. Here we saw our first black guillemots and black-legged kittiwakes. Kuttiwakes are small gull-like birds with black wing tips, legs and feet. They were nesting on the face of the cliffs. Each mossy cup was cemented to a tiny ledge high above the rolling sea. Rows of kittiwakes clung to the cliffs, some on nests, some sleeping, some just sitting. What a pre-

Though Bonaventure is best known for its gannets, we found black-legged kittiwakes (pictured), razorbills, common murres, black guillemots and common puffins also nesting there in large numbers.

carious existence, particularly for a chick!

By the time we completed the circle route, it was late afternoon. The provincial government requires that everyone be off the island by 5 P.M., when the last boat leaves for Percé. We just made it!

The next morning began with another early boat ride to the island. This time we took the first tourist cruise around the island for a look at the cliffs.

The tourist boats hold from 40 to 80 people and at the peak of the summer season leave the Percé dock every hour from 8

A.M. to 4 P.M. The small fee includes a tour past Percé Rock, around the cliffs at Bonaventure and, before returning to Percé, a stop at the Bonaventure dock for those who wish to walk on the island.

Before leaving Percé that second morning, we discussed our need for photographs with the boat captain. As it turned out, this was very helpful. He was kind enough to spend more than the usual amount of time at the best Bonaventure cliffs, allowing us to get the photos we wanted.

Equipped with a spare camera and lots of film, we drew near to the first cliff. It was a scene to remember forever. Up and down the face of this 200-foot precipice we saw thousands of birds—gannets, common murres, razorbills, black guillemots,

Tour boats to see the nesting cliffs leave Percé for Bonaventure Island every hour from 8 A.M. to 4 P.M. during the summer months. This boat ride alone is well worth a trip to the tip of Gaspé.

black-legged kittiwakes and herring gulls. Thousands upon thousands of them. Birds in the air, on the water, at the base of the cliffs, on the ledges, up and up and up to the top, more and more birds. The scene was too much to take in on one trip. We recommend you go at least twice, perhaps three times.

Even if you don't walk across the island to the upper gannet colony, it is worth all the trouble and effort it takes to get to Percé to make the boat trip around the cliffs. Surely this is one of the most dramatic spots in the bird world.

The Canadian Wildlife Service and the Quebec Provincial Government have done a commendable job of saving this seabird colony. The birds have made a strong comeback after dwindling to a few thousand in 1916. Disturbance from visitors has been alleviated by the new fence. But even though man is controlling egging and the killing of seabirds by direct causes, new and more subtle threats have arisen. Heavy use of DDT is suspected as the latest cause for a drop in the gannet population. In addition, small herring, the primary food of the gannets, are becoming increasingly scarce because of overfishing.

Not only at Bonaventure, but throughout the north Atlantic and north Pacific, it is increasingly difficult for seabirds to find food as the "mother lode" of herring is being fished out.

Thick-billed murres are having their own special problems. They are being killed by the thousands when they dive into gill nets set by Atlantic salmon fishermen.

Finally, the threat of oil spills increases daily as new rigs are built in the northern seas and oil tankers attending those rigs sail closer than ever to seabird colonies. Whole populations may be wiped out by a single accident.

As this book was being written, these facts about the increasing threats to our seabirds were just being revealed to the general public. We hope that an awakened public will help find solutions to these growing problems.

We were also concerned by the difficulty we had in purchasing fresh cod, salmon and other ocean fishes. We expected

As we passed the hole in Percé Rock en route to Bonaventure Island we watched gulls flying through it. A colony of great cormorants lives on the top of the rock.

Gaspé to be one of the best places in North America to buy seafood, but not so.

What we did find was great, but we discovered that fish were scarce and the future of the industry was not bright. This led us to conclude that the plight of the seabirds was also the plight of man.

VISITOR TIPS

Recommended time to visit: June–July.

Clothing: The weather was delightful while we were there, with only a sweater or light jacket needed occasionally. If you're going to walk on Bonaventure, we recommend comfortable walking shoes. All trails are easy to walk, although steep in some areas, and are well maintained, so hiking boots are not a necessity.

Lodging: Because Percé is a resort town, it has a number of motels.

Restaurants: Percé offers everything from hot dog stands to semi-formal restaurants.

Camping: There are two splendid government campgrounds in the village of Percé, one for tents only and one for RVs only.

Picnic Areas: If you're on Bonaventure, there are two areas for picnicking. One is at the beginning of the trail and the other is on the path to Gannet Colony Number 1. On the mainland, there is a picnic ground about one mile north of Percé on the main road (Highway 132).

Reservations: Very popular resort area; make reservations two to four weeks in advance. Write ahead for motel and camping information to:

> Centre d'Histoire Naturelle de Percé
> Percé, Comté Gaspé, Québec

Rest Rooms: On Bonaventure they are located at the beginning of the trail and at Gannet Colony Number 1.

Telephone: There is no public phone on Bonaventure, but there are a great many in Percé.

Gasoline: You'll find several service stations in Percé, but gasoline is expensive in Canada.

Groceries: We often shopped at the Co-op store on the wharf, where we were able to obtain fresh fish and all other food supplies we needed, but there are a number of small grocers in town. One good one is right outside the gate of the tent campground.

Hospital: Centre Hospital in the town of Gaspé.

Airport: There are no commercial airports close to Percé. The nearest ones are Presque Isle, Maine (U.S.A.), and Quebec City, Quebec (Canada).

Bird List: Pick up a checklist of 214 species while visiting the very fine Percé Wildlife Centre.

9

Hawk Mountain:
Sailors of the Mountaintops

Thousands of generations of birds of prey—sharp-shins, Cooper's hawks, goshawks, redtails, redshoulders, broadwings, falcons and eagles—have followed this express highway south. The hawk watcher sits on his boulder and glues his eyes to the sky. The long ridge, ablaze with autumn's reds and yellows, extends before us to the northeast. A sharp-eyed youngster is the first to spot a hawk. The boy calls out, "Hawk over hill number 3!" but leaves it to more experienced eyes to identify.

—Roger Tory Peterson

The spectacular autumn scene from Kittatinny Ridge in eastern Pennsylvania is reason enough for an annual pilgrimage to the top of Hawk Mountain. But the lure of tens of thousands of hawks to be seen winging their way south is irresistible in the hearts and minds of a legion of bird watchers whom one Hawk Mountain author refers to as the neomountain people.

As the sun moves south and the hours of daylight grow shorter, a cycle is triggered within every migratory bird which ends only with its death or its arrival at a predestined spot, perhaps as far away as South America, where it will spend the winter months.

The Atlantic Coast, the Great Lakes, major rivers and the Appalachian Mountains are the key landmarks in eastern North

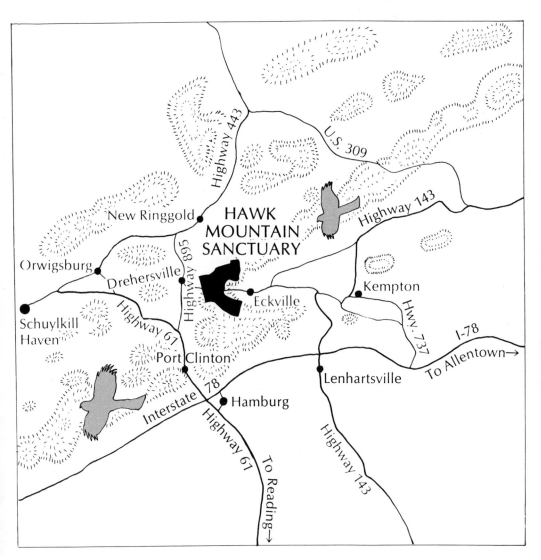

America that guide birds to their wintering grounds in the southern United States, Mexico, and Central and South America.

For thousands of years, raptors have used the lanes of the Appalachian Mountains both as a guidance system and as a magic carpet to ease their long flights south.

Perhaps more important than as a guide, the Appalachian

range offers the migrant raptors a free ride on the thermal air currents created by solar heating of the valleys and slopes or by the upward deflection of northwest winds. Hawks, eagles and falcons moving southward from Canada, New England and New York will cross many ridges, each with its own peculiar air currents. By favoring these currents, raptors conserve energy and muscle power needed to complete migratory flights of up to 4,500 miles. When conditions are right, birds will rise to tremendous heights and glide for hundreds of miles without so much as a single flap of their wings. The rising of many hawks together in a single swirling updraft is called "kettling." When the birds have spiraled to the necessary altitude, they will stream out of the kettle and glide south to the next thermal.

The Kittatinny is one of the best of the Appalachian ridges for numbers of hawk flights. Also, its many sandstone outcroppings are ideal places from which to watch the birds wing their way from the Catskills to the Susquehanna and southward. Midway between the gaps created in the Kittatinny by the Delaware and Susquehanna rivers is a bold outcropping known as the North Lookout of Hawk Mountain Sanctuary. It is here that the neomountain people gather each fall to watch the raptors flying by.

From past experience, I know that the best time to visit Hawk Mountain for the most spectacular flights is between September 15 and 20. It is during these five days that the number of broad-winged hawks usually reaches a peak. Broadwings are the only hawks that migrate in flocks. Hawks of other species travel alone or in small groups. Therefore, we scheduled our visit for September 17.

Weather conditions most favorable to a good flight are the same here as at Cape May, New Jersey—the passage of a low pressure system to the north over the New England states, an advancing cold front moving down from Canada and northwest winds for two or three consecutive days.

We were most fortunate—September 17 was one of those few "top days" at Hawk Mountain. When we arrived at the headquarters building at 9 A.M., the count reported by short-wave radio was already over 300. We quickly put on our hiking boots (good walking shoes are a must), paid our admission fee

Broadwings are the only hawks that migrate in large flocks. They often circle to great heights (kettling), then head south over Hawk Mountain on thermal air currents.

Hawk Mountain's North Lookout is the sanctuary's highest and best observation point. From here, the autumn ritual has been observed for a hundred years, first by men with guns and now by men with binoculars.

Visitors to Hawk Mountain's South Lookout focused on a "kettle" of broad-winged hawks as they rose on thermal air currents, their free ride south.

Beauty is all around at Hawk Mountain. In mid-September, mountain ash decorates the North Lookout, setting a foreground for the breathtaking view of the Schuylkill River Valley to the north.

($1 for adults, 50 cents for children) and started up the trail. (There are no rest rooms at the headquarters or at the top, so it is a good idea to stop at those along the trail at the foot of the mountain or halfway up the one-mile trail to the North Lookout.)

The first of the two best places to see hawks at Hawk Mountain is at the South Lookout, established in 1967 as an auxiliary observation point and convenient to the parking lot for elderly or handicapped visitors. The South Lookout is only a quarter mile up the somewhat rugged trail to the top. When we arrived there, some thirty hawk watchers were spotting new arrivals every few seconds. We were told that 162 broadwings had been counted in the past twenty minutes—it was shaping up as a good day.

During the next half hour we counted over 50 more broadwings and had a good visit with some old friends, including Curator Alex Nagy. Curious about events at the top, Kit and I followed the trail to the North Lookout.

At the halfway point we were given a choice: "Scenic Route This Way" or "Short Cut This Way." We were eager and took the shortcut. This express route to the top is no place for high-heeled shoes. Loose and often sharp rocks underfoot require sensible footwear. The shortcut was steep and not well defined.

As we approached the top, I had the same feeling I've had many times in the past. Because the rhododendron and mountain laurel are so thick, I feel that there must not be anyone at the lookout, but when we finally came onto the rocky outcrop, we were surprised to find about fifty hawk watchers clustered in groups of families and friends.

The view from the North Lookout is spectacular, especially when the coloring of autumn leaves is at a peak. One youngster is quoted as saying upon his arrival there, "Look, Mommy, the whole world!"

The North Lookout was a busy place most of the time we were there on September 17. It turned out to be one of the three best days of the year for hawk numbers. During our few hours we saw over 3,000 broadwings, a few sharpshins, marsh hawks (harriers), ospreys and American kestrels (sparrow hawks) and one goshawk.

One of 4,744 broadwings observed passing Hawk Mountain on a recent day. The peak of the broadwing flight is usually between September 15 and 20.

However, we nearly missed the big flight that day. As we were leaving, we heard some excitement and walked back to the lookout just in time to see one flock of 500 broadwings—the biggest flight of the day. During the next thirty minutes, we saw over 1,000 broadwings go by. One kettle alone contained 211 birds.

The procedure for identifying and counting hawks is well established. Observers sit on the rocks facing east watching a ridge with five knobs (humps) on it. The knobs are numbered 1 to 5, right to left. Most of the hawks are first seen above these stations. The first person to see a new hawk will call, "Bird over number three." Everyone looks at the new bird or birds and the official counter records the number and species.

It is important to tell you that none of the 3,000 broadwings which passed Hawk Mountain that day was close enough for good photographs. In fact, most were mere specks in the sky, flying at great heights over the lookout. It took a trained eye to make positive identifications of birds at those altitudes.

Visitors are warned not to expect birds in cages or a hawk in every tree. In fact, you are very lucky if birds fly close enough to you for good pictures. However, the earlier in the day you get there, the better are your chances. By afternoon, the thermals carry the birds to great heights—sometimes even out of sight for some observers.

Occasionally hawks do fly close—some even landing in nearby trees. When a bald eagle flew past the North Lookout only 30 yards from the nearest viewer, it was immediately dubbed "the bird of the year."

The neomountain people are relative newcomers to the rocky promontory at Hawk Mountain. Until 1934, mountain men of a different kind climbed to the overlook. These men carried shotguns and were determined to kill as many hawks as their supply of ammunition would permit.

A "good day's shooting" at Hawk Mountain before the area became a sanctuary in 1934.

Alex Nagy has worked at the Hawk Mountain Sanctuary for more than twenty years, first as a maintenance man and now as its Curator.

No one knows for sure when the first hawk shooters appeared on the mountain, but it had to be in the late 1800s or early 1900s. Regardless, when word got around, the "sport" of hawk shooting became popular. Records show that one man could shoot 500 rounds of ammunition, killing 200 or more birds, in a single day. Two guns were often used to keep one from getting too hot.

In 1932, Mrs. Rosalie Edge learned about the mass killings from Richard Pough, a Philadelphia news photographer who has since become a noted ornithologist. From her New York

City base, Mrs. Edge, chairman of the Emergency Conservation Committee, launched a campaign which culminated two years later in the purchase of 1,300 acres of land to establish the world's first sanctuary for the protection of migrating birds of prey.

The fact that the area became a sanctuary did not mean that the killing stopped immediately. It became obvious to Mrs. Edge that someone had to be at Hawk Mountain during the gunning season, so she hired Maurice Broun as the first curator. Broun and his devoted wife, Irma, spent thirty-two years at Hawk Mountain, creating a legend of themselves and an institution of the sanctuary. The Brouns retired in 1966 to nearby New Ringgold, where they could be close to the mountain while carrying on other conservation work.

Broun's successor, Alex Nagy, joined the Hawk Mountain staff in 1953 as a maintenance man. He has continued to work there for more than twenty years, first with the Brouns and since 1966 as Curator, swelling the Hawk Mountain Association membership to over 5,000.

Today, Alex Nagy and a staff of four, including Barbara Lake, a nine-year veteran of Hawk Mountain, supervise an enthusiastic conservation education program. Their new headquarters building, dedicated in 1974, could be a blueprint for any modern environmental nature center.

Hawk Mountain Sanctuary is open the year around, but is most popular between August and November when the hawks are flying. On a typical October weekend, more than 3,000 guests visit the sanctuary. The reported 50,000 visitors a year do not include 5,000 to 8,000 youngsters who use Hawk Mountain as an outdoor classroom. James Brett, education director, trains teachers, who in turn conduct their own classes in Hawk Mountain facilities.

Though I was never one of those students who visited the sanctuary with their classmates, I did see Hawk Mountain for the first time as a youngster during the late 1940s. Tagging along after my dad with oversize binoculars hanging heavy on my neck, I spent some glorious fall days perched on the rocks at the North Lookout. On one such occasion (perhaps my first trip), Dad and I visited with Roger Tory Peterson as we tallied

Turkey vultures are sometimes called "Kempton eagles" by old-timers at Hawk Mountain.

the passing raptors. I vividly recall the deep discussion between Dad and Roger over camera equipment and the techniques of nature photography. (Roger has become that extremely rare person in the nature field who is highly competent as photographer, writer and artist.)

My interest in Hawk Mountain continued as an adult. During the five and a half years I edited *Pennsylvania Game News*, I visited Hawk Mountain on a number of autumn days to renew my memories of the autumn pageant.

I recall that hawks, eagles and falcons were not the only birds seen at Hawk Mountain in the fall. Crows, ravens, turkey vultures (sometimes called "Kempton eagles" or "TVs" by veteran watchers), waterfowl and a great variety of songbirds also pass the lookouts.

I remember seeing great numbers of warblers on one of my visits as a youth. Magnolias, yellowrumps (myrtles) and Nashvilles, I believe, were the most common. It was not unusual to see ruby-throated hummingbirds zip by and great numbers of monarch butterflies sail along on the breezes.

It was no surprise, then, that Roger Peterson listed Hawk Mountain in September as one of his dozen best birding hot spots in North America.

Though the great flights of broadwings can be observed only during September, there are other good flights to be seen at Hawk Mountain. In late September, hundreds of American kestrels (sparrow hawks) and ospreys come through. Early October brings thousands of sharpshins, while late October is the time for red-tailed, red-shouldered and marsh hawks (harriers). November is highlighted with more buteos plus golden eagles, goshawks, and rare rough-legged hawks from the Arctic. Bald eagles are more often seen in August and September, peaking around Labor Day.

If you have only one week to devote to hawk watching, do as we did—go there in the middle of September.

Cape May, New Jersey, is also at its peak during this same period, so we decided to devote nearly two weeks to the two areas. On September 18 the weather turned cloudy and rainy. Despite the bad weather, 875 hawks, mostly broadwings and sharpies, were recorded. At one period during this day, we were two of only four people at the North Lookout. The 19th was a complete disaster with more rain and fog, so we moved on to Cape May, intending to return to Hawk Mountain the following week.

Ideal weather conditions for a super flight hit Cape May and Hawk Mountain on the same Monday morning, September 22. While we were having the birding of a lifetime in New Jersey (see Cape May chapter), those at Hawk Mountain recorded 4,744 broadwings—one of the best days in recent history. Too bad we couldn't be at both places at the same time!

Knowledge of the big days at both Cape May and Hawk Mountain on September 22 reinforces a well-known fact: specific weather conditions are vital to a good migration. Apparently September 22 was perfect for the migration of birds throughout eastern North America. The challenge is to anticipate these conditions and then be at the right location to experience the phenomenon. Both Hawk Mountain and Cape May Point are the right locations. Mid-September is the right time. As to the exact date—well, you have to take it from there. One day can make a difference.

The following day, September 23, was the day Hurricane Eloise moved in and shut down both Hawk Mountain and Cape May for bird watching.

The second-most-common hawk at Hawk Mountain is the sharpshin. Sharpies migrate from late September to mid-October. More than 8,000 have been seen there in recent years.

During the hurricane weather, however, one of the assistant curators at Hawk Mountain, Mike Heller, donned two raincoats and sloshed up to the South Lookout for 1½ hours. Surprisingly, he saw 146 broadwings, most of which were close enough for him to count feathers. They actually alighted in the trees around him. So bad weather doesn't necessarily mean no hawks.

Unusual happenings are somewhat common at Hawk Mountain. For example, there was a day in 1974 when 3 different species of eagles were seen. Since there are only 2 well-known species of eagles in North America, one would have to

Perhaps the most sought-after bird at Hawk Mountain is the peregrine falcon. This endangered species has never been common at Hawk Mountain, but hit a peak of 44 in 1941. In recent years that number has dwindled to less than 20 each year.

be skeptical. However, a tawny eagle with jesses (straps) on its legs was seen at Hawk Mountain on the same day that both bald and golden eagles had been recorded. It was later discovered that the tawny, a native of Africa and Asia, had escaped in Philadelphia some six months earlier. And on a day in 1959 following a hurricane, the sighting was reported of a Kermadec petrel from the South Pacific.

Many of the unusual events at Hawk Mountain concern people, not birds. No fewer than four marriages have taken place at the North Lookout. One wedding party carried their formal wear up the mountain in paper bags, changing clothes in the upper rest rooms. Alex Nagy received a radio call from the top which went something like this: "Alex, you'll never guess what is happening up here. We're having a wedding, complete with preacher and wedding party." Alex never did figure out which group it was, because they changed into hiking clothes before returning to the bottom of the mountain.

On another occasion, Nagy reports that a car drove up with a family in it and the middle-aged man who was driving asked Alex if he had seen his mother! A brief explanation revealed that the mother was none other than sixty-nine-year-old Mrs. Emma Gatewood, the famous Appalachian Trail walker. Mrs. Gatewood's son knew the Appalachian Trail crossed Hawk Mountain and wanted to intercept her there. Apparently Mrs. Gatewood had ignored her family's opposition to her walking the trail at that age. (She had walked the entire trail at age sixty-seven.) They did intercept her, but were not successful in dissuading her. She walked the entire length of the trail once again. She walked another trail from Independence, Missouri, to Portland, Oregon, at seventy-one.

Nagy told us about an elderly woman who phoned Hawk Mountain regarding her sister's last will and testament. The deceased sister had been an actress of some fame, and her last request was to be cremated and have her ashes spread by an eagle. The caller wanted to know if Hawk Mountain had any eagles who would spread the ashes.

The woman apparently didn't know that eagles merely pass over Hawk Mountain . . . and fewer today than ever before. No sooner had the hawk gunners been silenced throughout North

Mid-October is the best time to see marsh hawks passing Hawk Mountain.

America than a new and far greater threat appeared. The mass use of DDT reduced the numbers of many birds of prey. Bald eagles were among the hardest hit. In 1950, watchers saw as many as 142 bald eagles. Only 25 to 30 have been recorded in recent years. The bald eagle, a fish eater, obtains much of its food by picking up weakened or injured prey. In recent years, the ailing fish have often been those suffering from the effects of chemicals. This selective feeding process has backfired on the predator.

Other raptor species gravely affected by DDT are the peregrine falcon, Cooper's hawk and osprey. Strangely, the osprey numbers at Hawk Mountain do not reflect an osprey problem, perhaps because those flying over Hawk Mountain are from fresh-water areas, whereas the ospreys hardest hit are those that feed near salt water.

Nevertheless, with the ban on DDT, some increases have already been noted, but not significant enough to be decisive at this time. A late letter from Alex Nagy reported 1975 totals of over 31,000 birds, the second-highest count in Hawk Mountain history.

Nagy noted a dramatic increase in the number of butterflies in the Hawk Mountain area. Butterflies may be better indicators of the health of our environment than birds.

In any event, Hawk Mountain Sanctuary is one of the truly great birding spots in North America. As someone quipped to a questioning reporter recently, "Hawk Mountain is the only place in the world where people willingly donate $1 to $100 just for the privilege of sitting on a hard rock in the rain!"

VISITOR TIPS

Recommended time to visit: September 17 to 25.

Clothing: Plan your clothing as you would for any fall outing in the Northeast. But good, sturdy walking shoes or hiking boots are important.

Lodging: Pottsville and Schuylkill Haven, to the north, have several motels. There are also motels in Hamburg, Lenhartsville and Krumsville and along Interstate 78.

Restaurants: The closest restaurants are in New Ringgold, Kempton, Hamburg, Lenhartsville, Shartlesville and Orwigsburg, as well as east on I-78. If we're planning to spend the day on the mountain we always pack a lunch; we hate to come down the mountain to drive to a restaurant and risk missing something.

Camping: No camping is allowed on the sanctuary, but there are at least three campgrounds within a short drive of the sanctuary—two in Lenhartsville and one in Auburn. They have facilities for RVs as well as tents.

Picnic Areas: You may picnic at either lookout, but you must take your trash along with you when you leave. Leaser Lake, about 5 miles to the west, has a picnic area with tables.

Reservations: We had no problems with accommodations, and advance reservations are probably not needed. For information on motels and camping accommodations, write to:

> Hawk Mountain Sanctuary
> Route 2
> Kempton, Pennsylvania 19529

Rest Rooms: None in the headquarters building or at the lookouts— only at the bottom of the mountain and about halfway to the top.

Telephone: Although the headquarters does not have a public phone, the Hawk Mountain personnel would allow the use of their telephone in the event of an emergency.

Gasoline: Drehersville, Port Clinton and Kempton have gasoline.

Groceries: Kempton, Drehersville, Schuylkill Haven and Pottsville.

Hospital: Pottsville is the closest, but Reading and Allentown also have hospitals.

Airport: Allentown or Reading.

Bird List: A list of 296 species is available at headquarters, where you can also buy copies of *Feathers in the Wind.* This book by James Brett and Alex Nagy will give you a good background to make your Hawk Mountain visit even more enjoyable.

10

Cape May:

The Morning of Birding Madness

At daybreak, near Cape May Light, I have watched small birds, weak and tired, beating their way in over the surf, tacking into the stiff northwesterly breeze that had carried them offshore. The number of birds that pass by some mornings is incredible—10,000 robins, 5,000 flickers, several thousands of yellow-rumped (myrtle) warblers; blackbirds and meadowlarks by the hundreds. I have counted a thousand sharp-shinned hawks in a morning from the concrete highway where it passes through the pine woods.

—*Roger Tory Peterson*

"If you have a really *good* day at Cape May, it will be the best birding day of your life. If you have a really *great* day, it will be one of the worst birding days of your life—that is, it will be so frustrating to try to see and identify all the birds around you that you will nearly go mad!"

These were the words of New York State Assemblyman Robert J. Connor, a twenty-three-year veteran of the Cape May autumn birding phenomenon.

"On the 'mad days,'" Connor continued, "birds are hanging on the bushes and shrubs and literally cover the ground. There are so many birds you just can't believe it."

During Connor's twenty-three years of autumn fieldwork, he has spent forty-two days birding at Cape May during peak

The lighthouse at Cape May Point is a landmark for man. The point of land it marks presents a dilemma for migrating birds. To continue south, they must strike out over 18 miles of open water to Delaware.

periods. Many of these were *good* days and three were *great* days.

When we met Bob Connor on September 21, he had been at Cape May and Brigantine (50 miles north) for nearly a week and had listed 154 species. By the end of the week, he was to have 160. He had kept detailed records during fifteen fall flights since 1952, and told us that his best bird list totaled 170 species during four days in 1968.

Connor's experiences and many others like them are what brought Kit and me to southern New Jersey on this date.

Many of the birds throughout northeastern North America favor the Atlantic Coast for their autumn flight south. Songbirds,

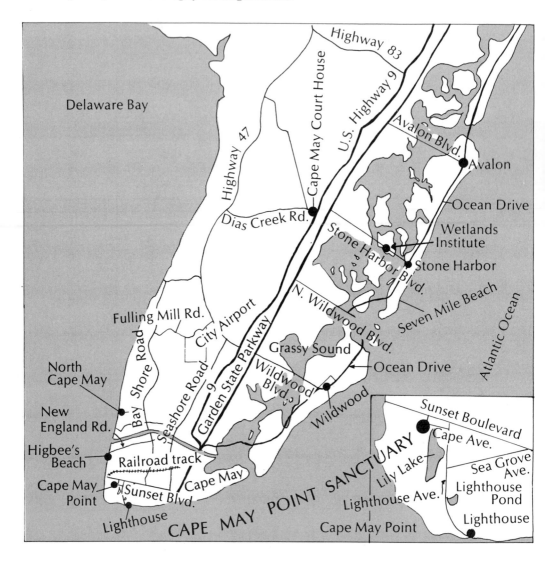

birds of prey, waterfowl and shore birds use the same routes to pour out of the Maritime Provinces, the New England states and the mid-Atlantic states. Water—first the creeks and rivers and then the seacoast—seems to guide them. Down they come by the millions, increasing in numbers as they migrate south along the Jersey shore. Depending on weather and wind direction, some years they come through New Jersey in dramatic waves. In other years, they are more dispersed.

When the birds reach Cape May, the southernmost tip of New Jersey, they face extreme difficulties. To continue south, they must strike out over Delaware Bay, a flight of 18 miles over open water. If there is a strong northwest wind, crossing the open water may mean death, because the wind could blow the birds helplessly out to sea. At times like these, the birds stack up at the Cape and produce the "days of madness" that Bob Connor described. They either wait at the Point for improved weather or mill around the communities of Stone Harbor, Cape May and Cape May Point. Often a bird that tries to cross the bay against strong winds is forced back and sits exhausted on the first perch it finds.

Connor's *good* days, however, are different. They follow a front that has brought in good weather. The birds are moving through the Cape in great numbers and, with only a little hesitation, head over the bay for Delaware.

The southern tip of New Jersey is a paradox of well-settled communities and well-preserved native wild lands. This stretch of Seven Mile Beach with the condominiums of Wildwood in the background is an example.

At the peak of the frenzy at Cape May Point, rose-breasted grosbeaks (like the one pictured), flickers, red-breasted nuthatches and a half dozen warblers were flying through in droves.

The fraternal feeling among bird watchers was evident that Sunday afternoon when we met Bob Connor. As we pulled up to this binocular-clad man leaning against his green station wagon, he smiled at us and asked if we had seen all the falcons flying over. Having just arrived, we pleaded ignorance. Connor told us that the day's weather was ideal for a big flight that night and the next morning. The passing of many merlins (pigeon hawks) over the point was further evidence that conditions were right for a *good* day.

That evening we drove to the lighthouse at Cape May Point

to check on night-flying birds. Most migrants fly at night if weather conditions are right. Though there was no big flight evident, we did hear an occasional chip or peep overhead.

At dawn the next morning, September 22, Kit and I were standing on Cape May Point in the little thicket of bayberry, red cedar and holly at the corner of Sunset Boulevard and Cape Avenue (at the head of Lily Lake). As we approached the area we knew it was going to be an exceptional morning. Every few yards, birds crossed the road ahead of our car. By the time we parked, we were adding new species faster than Kit could write.

"Rose-breasted grosbeak, redstart, scarlet tanager, mockingbird, red-breasted nuthatch, black-and-white warbler," I called to her.

The big problem was getting our binoculars on each bird before it flew on. They were all in a hurry and were hesitating only long enough to grab an insect, a berry or a seed.

"That looked like a black-throated blue, but I didn't get a good look at it."

"If you haven't seen a flicker yet, there are 6 over here right now."

"You'll never believe what I have over here. A lark sparrow!"

"Hey, look up there. A sparrow hawk and a blue jay flying side by side."

In less than an hour, Kit and I listed 46 species, including 14 warblers. At Lily Lake we found black ducks, mallards, American widgeon (baldpates), a single snow goose, herring and laughing gulls and several snowy egrets.

At times, songbirds were so numerous and moving so swiftly that on separate occasions Kit and I were almost hit by a low-flying Swainson's (olive-backed) thrush, a common yellow-throat and a tree swallow.

An interesting point about the direction of flight was that the birds flying through the thickets at the head of Lily Lake were flying *north*. Apparently they had followed the coast south around Cape May Point and then continued to follow the curve north up the western shore, at least as far as Higbee's Beach, rather than head out over Delaware Bay at the Point.

Opposite: The local mockingbirds seemed disoriented by the thousands of other songbirds pushing through their territory at Cape May Point.

There were so many Swainson's thrushes that we nearly got hit several times as they moved through the thickets at Cape May Point.

A lone snow goose found Lily Lake at Cape May Point a good place to feed and rest before moving south.

Below: A snowy egret poised to strike at a minnow at the edge of Lily Lake on Cape May Point during the peak migration.

When Bob Connor (right) joined us at Cape May Point on the "big day," he was with three Englishmen who had flown over just to be at Cape May for the migration.

The woodlands along Lighthouse Avenue at Cape May Point are a real "hot spot" on a good birding day in September.

One of the best places to see migrating raptors is at Cape May Point State Park near the U.S. Coast Guard Station. On the day of the big flight we joined these birders from northern New Jersey as they watched American kestrels, sharp-shins and marsh hawks sail by.

Another interesting feature about birding at Cape May was the fact that we were surrounded by houses, roads and even kids waiting for school buses. Most of Cape May is well settled, but birds continue to follow the ancient migration route through the now suburban setting. Indeed, the area where we were seeing so many birds is a picnic area maintained by the Borough of Cape May Point.

At about 8:30 A.M., Bob Connor appeared with three English birders. The young men had flown from Great Britain just to experience the Cape May spectacle. They had been birding at the base of the lighthouse most of the morning and reported that several species of hawks had been seen. We drove the few blocks around Lily Lake and into the parking lot next to the lighthouse. From there we walked into Cape May Point State Park and crossed an open field to an old concrete foundation. We joined a couple from northern New Jersey who pointed out American kestrels (sparrow hawks) and sharp-shinned and marsh hawks as the raptors glided on thermal currents over the Point. Aside from the hawks, very little was seen at the lighthouse, so we moved to the wooded areas along both Lighthouse and Sea Grove avenues.

Some of the Spanish oak, sweet gum, holly and swamp maple woodlands have been preserved as an Audubon Sanctuary and some by the State of New Jersey through the Green Acres program. Our walks along Lighthouse and Sea Grove avenues produced more songbirds: gray catbirds; brown thrashers; cardinals; black-throated green, yellow-rumped (myrtle), Canada and Wilson's warblers; yellow-billed cuckoos; Carolina wrens and many others.

Tree swallows were congregating between the lighthouse and Lily Lake. At one point during the morning there were several thousand on the telephone wires near Lighthouse Pond. At another time they were swarming on the wires in a residential area near the beach. We had heard that during the previous week, the tree swallows were so thick over Wildwood, New Jersey, that they darkened the skies and made tourists uneasy.

There have been some rarities seen at Cape May through the years. Four wood ibis were once spotted at Lighthouse Pond, and Julian Potter and William Baily recorded a Mississippi kite on the road to Higbee's Beach on another occasion.

Identifying birds during fall migration is far more difficult than during the spring. Most birds stop singing in late summer. Therefore, when they pass through Cape May in the fall, they move quickly and quietly.

Furthermore, many have changed plumages to duller, less distinct attire. For example the rose-breasted grosbeak had lost most of its rose breast. The male scarlet tanager was no longer scarlet; it was lemon-colored like the female. The "confusing

Later in the morning of the big day at Cape May, we caught this broadwing resting above Sunset Boulevard near Lighthouse Avenue.

Thousands of tree swallows congregated between the lighthouse and Sea Grove Avenue on Cape May Point.

Semipalmated plovers were common along Seven Mile Beach the day after the hurricane.

fall warblers" are always difficult, and it takes more than a casual glance to identify many of them.

Songbirds are not the only ones with confusing fall plumages. On an afternoon stroll down Seven Mile Beach near Stone Harbor with Pennsylvania friends Viv and Will Johns, we sorted out the difficult fall identification marks for piping and semipalmated plovers as well as sanderlings, semipalmated sandpipers and laughing gulls.

One large flock of sanderlings intrigued us with the pattern of their movements on the wet beach against a background of foamy white breakers. The flow of hundreds of sanderlings looked like a stream of white water running along the incoming tide.

We were also impressed by the migration of monarch butterflies. Like the birds, they follow the coast as they flit their way south. Monarchs were everywhere on Cape May, but nowhere was their countless procession as evident as over the sand dunes at Seven Mile Beach.

Just like the birds, monarch butterflies follow the Atlantic shoreline as they migrate south. We saw thousands of them flitting over the sand dunes.

We were intrigued by the sanderlings on Seven Mile Beach. Each time a wave rolled in they ran back, much like kids not wanting to get wet.

There were so many interesting sights on the beach that day that no matter what your interest in the outdoors might be, there was something for you. If we had been at Cape May to fish, for example, Seven Mile Beach would have been our hot spot that day. The thirty surf fishermen lined up near the Stone Harbor point were striking it rich with bluefish. Some were using mullet chunks as bait; others used artificial plugs; but everyone, including some youngsters, was catching 1½- to 3-pound blues. If you have ever eaten fresh bluefish, you'll know why I was tempted to put birding aside for a few hours.

After watching the bluefish fishermen we drove to the Stone Harbor Bird Sanctuary a few blocks away. This 21-acre stand of natural beach woodland was set aside in 1947 as a bird sanctuary by the Borough of Stone Harbor. It is heavily used as a breeding rookery in the summer months by egrets, herons and ibis. During the other months, the birds roost and feed in the sanctuary. It was here that we saw our first glossy ibis.

When Charles Lindbergh visited the Stone Harbor Bird Sanctuary some years ago, he made these comments:

> . . . how interesting I found the early-dawn flights of the birds to be—the mist of wings rising from tree branches—the filtering upward of more feathered bodies through the leaves—the seemingly endless supply of birds, as though they were emerging from the earth itself.

During our first twenty-four hours, and before the arrival of Hurricane Eloise, we listed 90 species. The storm forced us indoors for two days while 7 inches of rain drenched southern New Jersey. The hurricane interrupted the flow of birds, and we found pickin's a little slim for the remainder of our stay.

Our visit to Cape May was actually a revisit for me. I had accompanied my father there on a field trip in 1952. One of the memorable experiences of that earlier trip was seeing New Jersey's first cattle egret at the Michael McPherson farm, on the road to Higbee's Beach. Kit and I went to Higbee's Beach after the storm and on the way found dozens of cattle egrets mingling with horses, sheep and cattle. This immigrant species has done well on our continent.

Higbee's Beach produced more birds of prey. American

In 1952, I saw the first cattle egret reported in New Jersey. Today that same area on the road to Higbee's Beach is well populated with the descendants of that first pioneer.

kestrels and sharp-shinned hawks were following the shoreline. We watched 2 different sharpshins pick off songbirds while sailing over wooded areas. One sharpy demonstrated its keen eyesight by dropping several hundred feet to strike an unsuspecting warbler.

Between Cape May Point and Higbee's Beach is a railroad track worth walking. The tracks from Bayshore Road to the magnesite factory off Sunset Boulevard produced a dozen new species for us, including a female ruby-throated hummingbird which was number 100 on our list. We watched a covey of 12

The railroad track between Cape May Point and Higbee's Beach was well worth walking. We added a dozen new species there, including a covey of bobwhites.

From the observation tower at the Wetlands Institute at Stone Harbor we got an excellent view of a saltwater marsh and many water birds feeding there.

bobwhites cross the tracks, chortling as they disappeared into cover.

Another worthwhile stop was the Wetlands Institute at Stone Harbor. This research unit of Lehigh University affords an excellent view of the salt marshes from an observation tower. Gaining sufficient altitude to photograph the salt marshes has always been a problem for me, but the Institute tower took care of that.

Some days we birded along the Garden State Parkway and Ocean Drive from Cape May through Wildwood to Stone Harbor. On stretches between the communities, we found salt-marsh birding excellent from both roads. At Grassy Sound Bridge, along Ocean Drive, we watched tree swallows swarming in the 10-foot-tall phragmites, and over the toll bridge laughing gulls hung motionless on the air as if suspended by invisible wires. A little farther along, we watched a herring gull drop a quahog clam on the concrete road—its way of cracking the shell.

Roger Tory Peterson first visited Cape May nearly fifty years ago as a teen-ager. He and two of his buddies thumbed their way to the Cape for their first great birding adventure.

During the intervening years, Peterson has watched the changes in the bird populations and considers Cape May and Hawk Mountain to be barometers of the health of our overall environment. During the mid-'30s, Peterson went to Cape May to witness the slaughter of hawks by gunners. In the 1950s and 1960s, he monitored the drastic reduction of hawks due to the saturation of our environment by DDT and other chlorinated hydrocarbons.

Recalling an experience with the hawk shooters in 1935, Peterson wrote:

> At Cape May, as at Hawk Mountain, the hawks were slaughtered for years before anyone became concerned. A concrete highway runs from east to west through the groves of Spanish oaks just north of the town of Cape May Point. Here the local gunners formerly lined the road and waited for the hawks to come over. One September morning in 1935, I watched 800 sharpshins try to cross the firing line. Each time a "sharpy" sailed over the treetops it was met by a pattern of lead. Some

folded up silently; others, with head wounds, flopped to the ground, chattering shrilly. By noon 254 birds lay on the pavement.

That evening, in a Cape May home, I sat down to a meal of hawks—twenty sharpshins, boiled like squabs, for a family of six. I tasted the birds, found them good, and wondered what my friends would say if they could see me. Like a spy breaking bread with the enemy, I felt uneasy. I could not tell my hosts I disapproved, for their consciences were clear—weren't they killing the hawks as edible game and at the same time saving all the little songbirds? It would have done no good to explain predation, ecology and the natural balance to these folks. Having lived at Cape May all their lives, they had a distorted idea of the abundance of hawks. They did not realize that a single season's sport by the Cape May gunners could drain the sharpshins from thousands of square miles of northern woodlands.

Since Peterson wrote these paragraphs, model laws have been passed in New Jersey, Pennsylvania and most other states to protect all birds of prey.

During the 1950s and 1960s, Peterson's concern for the contamination of the environment was dramatized by the severe drop in the numbers of birds of prey passing over Cape May and Hawk Mountain. About this he wrote:

The thing that disturbs me most is not that a million songbirds should die with DDT tremors, upsetting though it may be. We still have a great many warblers and robins. Their reproductive potential is high, and they will probably survive until we get some sense and the hydrocarbon syndrome is a thing of the past.

I am more concerned about those species that are at the ends of the long food chains—particularly bird-eating birds and certain of the fish-eating birds that eat large fish. A lifetime of observation in many parts of the world and in every state of the union has convinced me that those species are in the greatest danger and some may even face eventual extinction.

Peterson's fears were well founded. It's possible that the ban on DDT and similar compounds has saved most of the birds

On the day Hurricane Eloise passed, we were busy on the beaches of Cape May photographing and recording the new birds brought in by the storm.

of prey. Unfortunately, it came too late for the eastern race of the peregrine falcon.

Other famous ornithologists are associated with Cape May. Most prominent was Witmer Stone (1866–1930), whose two-volume work *Bird Studies at Old Cape May* is still the most valuable reference for birding. During the hurricane, Kit and I passed the time by reading these fine old books.

Admittedly, Hurricane Eloise put a damper on our Cape May visit, but we felt fortunate to have witnessed the big flight on our first morning. Of all the birding we did for this book, no one hour was filled with more excitement than the onslaught of songbirds pouring out of the thickets that Monday morning. We listed most of our 105 species before noon that day. If we had been able to identify every bird we saw, I'm sure our list would have been over 150.

A letter from Bob Connor several weeks later reinforced our opinion about the heavy flight:

> That Monday morning, September 22, was fabulous. My day's count, 120, was lower than my record, 128, but the latter was a full day's birding, while this year included only a very hurried trip through Brigantine. Additionally, not knowing that I was on the way to such a day, I didn't bother to even look for some of the obvious—like coot or barn swallow. In retrospect, I'm sure if I had stayed all day I would have easily passed 130. But that's the charm of it . . . I have it to do next time.

VISITOR TIPS

Recommended time to visit: September 15 to 25.

Note: Unlike any other birding hot spot covered in this book, the Cape May area is heavily populated and dotted with small communities. Therefore, facilities for eating, sleeping, etc., are numerous.

Clothing: Temperatures can be cool, but might also get into the 80s. You should have comfortable walking shoes.

Lodging: There is an abundance of accommodations through Cape May County, but many close for the season after Labor Day, so it would be a good idea to write for a list of motels that will be open during your visit.

Restaurants: Many restaurants close after Labor Day, but we had no problem finding a great many that remain open all year.

Camping: There are dozens of private campgrounds, but here again, we'd suggest you make arrangements before you arrive.

Picnic Areas: A small picnic area is located at the head of Lily Lake in Cape May Point. You may also picnic on the beaches.

Reservations: Reservations should be made at least two weeks in advance, not because the facilities will be crowded but because many businesses in Cape May County close after Labor Day. Write for motel, hotel and camping information to:

> Cape May Board of Chosen Freeholders
> P.O. Box 365
> Cape May Court House, New Jersey 08210
> (609) 465-7111
>
> Cape May County Chamber of Commerce
> Box 74
> Cape May Court House, New Jersey 08210

Rest Rooms: The Wetlands Institute was the only birding spot that offered public rest rooms.

Telephone: Almost all of the communities in Cape May County have public telephones.

Gasoline: Gas is available in nearly all the towns in this area.

Groceries: Supermarkets or small grocery stores can be found in almost any of the towns.

Hospital: Cape May Court House.

Airport: There is a small county airport west of Cape May, but the closest one for commercial flights is in Atlantic City.

Bird List: There are no printed checklists given out anywhere in the county. We used "A Field List of Birds of the Delaware Valley Region," available from the Delaware Valley Ornithological Club, Academy of Natural Sciences, Philadelphia.

11

Horicon:

At the Sign of the Flying Goose

The largest concentration of Canada geese on the continent attracts so many weekend goose watchers that traffic police must handle the crowds. Hundreds of cars line the highway across the marsh and it is a moot question as to which is the more remarkable spectacle, the geese or the people.

—*Roger Tory Peterson*

Imagine, if you can, Canada geese as far as you can see. Some flying, some walking, most of them grazing. All in small family groups, all talking at once.

Every fall since the early 1970s there have been over 200,000 Canada geese at Horicon National Wildlife Refuge in east-central Wisconsin. That total is more Canada geese than have ever before been assembled on the North American continent.

The geese are so numerous in the Horicon Marsh area that a visitor can be assured of seeing large numbers of geese on any autumn day, rain or shine.

"During the months of October and November, it is impossible to look in any direction during daylight hours within one

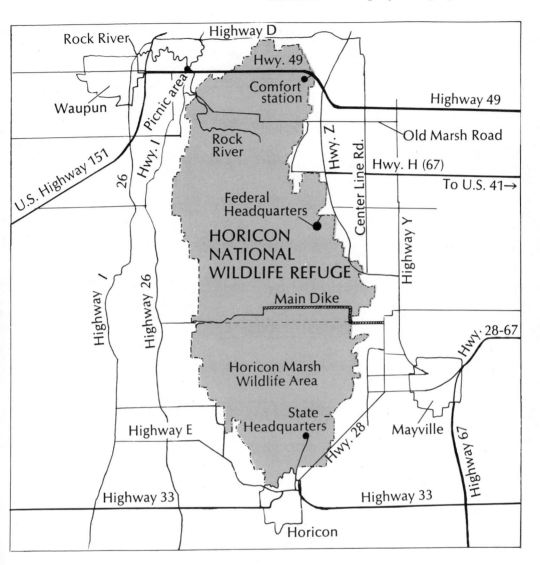

mile of the federal refuge and not see geese," boldly claimed
former Refuge Manager Robert Personius.

The best place at Horicon to see geese at close range is
from State Route 49 just east of the community of Waupun
where the highway traverses the northern tip of the refuge.
Route 49 has become quite an attraction for "goose lookers" in

October in east-central Wisconsin means apples, honey, sausage, cheese and the sounds and sights of flying geese.

recent years. On Saturdays and Sundays in October there will be as many as 30,000 people traveling that 2-mile stretch of road (weekdays are not crowded). The Fish and Wildlife Service has taken advantage of this public attraction and stations information officers on the highway to talk with visitors about the geese. By the fall of 1976, a new tour road through the refuge will be completed.

The Horicon Refuge is the most familiar to us of all the birding hot spots because it is only 50 miles from our home. During my ten years in Wisconsin I have gone to the 21,000-acre federal refuge several times each year and have followed the goose situation very closely.

We like Horicon best in early October, though the geese are there in great numbers from mid-September to early December. But in early October, we find a unique mixture of late-summer weather, brilliant autumn colors and goose numbers at

On an average Saturday or Sunday at Horicon in October, 18,000 to 20,000 cars filled with eager goose lookers file across Route 49 east of Waupun.

their peak. What is more beautiful than to follow a V of honkers from a deep blue sky across an orange woodlot and into a field of golden grain?

Early October is good for birding also because the hunting season has not started and the geese and other waterfowl are less nervous and easier to approach for photographs.

October in Wisconsin is the time for apples, honey, sausage and the world's finest cheese. It's a great time to travel in Wisconsin and a great time to be alive.

When Kit and I drive to Horicon, we usually go north on U.S. Route 41 until we reach either Route 28, 67 or 49 going west. Any of these roads takes us to the marsh, each offering a slightly different scene as it approaches through Wisconsin farmland. On one of our many trips to the marsh this year we were accompanied by my parents. On that day, October 14, we selected Route 28, which took us past the Theresa Marsh, a state-managed wetlands about a mile west of Route 41. We stopped at the observation point and tallied the birds sitting on and around the ponds: water (American) pipits, common (Wilson's) snipes, killdeers, dunlins, red-tailed hawks, black ducks, mallards and gadwalls, cowbirds, rusty blackbirds and common (purple) grackles. The water level in these ponds is controlled by pumping. The area is planted in grain in the spring and reflooded in the fall. Later that day at Horicon we saw dowitchers, savannah sparrows, pied-billed grebes, tree swallows, ring-necked pheasants and snow geese, in addition to the hordes of Canada geese.

On another visit this year, we were in the company of a most distinguished birder.

"There goes a shrike," yelled one of the graduate students in the back seat.

"I hope it's a northern," I responded. "Kit and I haven't seen a northern shrike this year and we'd like to add it to our book list."

My companion remained silent as he watched the shrike through his binoculars. We all waited for a pronouncement. Was it a loggerhead or a northern shrike? No one in the car was about to identify it until Roger Tory Peterson spoke.

"The difference in the two shrikes is the light area above

As long as the Horicon grainfields hold up along Route 49, geese were easy to see only a few feet from the highway. Later in the season, they foraged on private land.

On his recent visit to Horicon, Roger Tory Peterson photographed a huge flock of geese as they rose from one of many refuge ponds.

Roger Tory Peterson with a crippled goose at Horicon. Cripples are cared for by refuge personnel or given to zoos.

the black mask, lighter lower mandible and faintly barred breast of the northern," Roger told us. Still no one ventured a guess.

"Who has a field guide?" I asked. No one in our vehicle had a Peterson *Field Guide*. After all, who needed one with the man right there? Kit was with Peg and Joe Hickey in the car next to us. All three looked at me strangely as I called to them for a field guide.

"You want to refresh your memory visually?" Roger asked me politely.

"Yes; I'm hazy on the difference in the two shrikes and I need to see the book."

"It's always good to see the field marks in the guide as well as talk about them," he reassured me.

A quick look at the Hickeys' copy of the Peterson guide brought back to my mind the diagnostic markings of the two shrikes. We all agreed that the bird we were looking at was indeed a northern shrike.

Roger Peterson had come to Horicon to see the geese, but as we toured the refuge we also saw many other species, including rusty and red-winged blackbirds, white-throated and fox sparrows, yellow-rumped (myrtle) warblers, both green-winged and blue-winged teal, black ducks, mallards, gadwalls, American widgeon (baldpates), northern shovelers and great blue herons.

One morning in early October, I accompanied Dr. Howard Lee of Milwaukee to the refuge. Dr. Lee has taken more photographs of Canada geese in flight than any other man I know. After shooting a couple of hundred pictures of honkers coming in to the cornfield behind Federal Headquarters, Howard suggested that we get permission to move through the standing corn to the far edge to get some close-ups of the feeding geese. When we entered the field we were unaware that hundreds of geese were feeding in the standing corn. We could not see them, and they could not see us. As we walked across the rows of corn, surprised geese began to flush. First a few dozen, then a hundred or more, and finally the sky was filled with flapping honkers struggling to become airborne. The big birds made unbelievably loud noises as their flailing wings crashed against the dry cornstalks. What an experience!

Almost all the geese in that field, indeed in all of Horicon, were *Branta canadensis interior* (Todd's goose), one of the 15 known subspecies of Canada geese. The Horicon variety is a middle-sized Canada goose, though a few of the larger and smaller subspecies are mixed in.

The scene that unfolded as Dr. Lee and I walked through the cornfield will remain with me for the rest of my life.

Every year, a few thousand snow geese (including some of the blue phase) and white-fronted geese are seen with the Canadas. Some years such unusual birds as brant, bar-headed geese and Canada–snow goose hybrids are reported. This year there was an albino Canada in the flock. There have been other unusual sightings, like the Canada goose seen wearing a plastic six-pack holder around its neck.

Aldo Leopold once wrote, "What a dull world if we knew all about geese!" Nevertheless, this year about 1,200 honkers were wearing brightly colored collars as research markers. Biologists hope to find out more about their movements by keeping track of the marked birds as they come and go to and from the refuge. We still have much to learn to better manage geese.

The subspecies of Canada goose most common at Horicon is Todd's goose, a middle-sized bird among the other subspecies of honkers.

We do know that the Horicon geese have a feeling of security inside the refuge. I have watched them become vastly wilder creatures as they pass over the boundary line into farm fields. By contrast, on Route 49 the big birds display a carefree attitude toward humans and it is easy to get within a few yards of the closest without alarming them.

A Canada goose family consists of from 2 to 9 birds. A mated pair may have as many as 4 goslings with them from this year's nesting and as many as 3 from last year's brood. A goose does not breed until it is two or even three years old. At that age it mates, and it retains the same mate till one of the pair dies. The average life span is about five years, although some have lived to be thirty.

Each goose is a master of the airways. Depending on wind and altitude, a Canada goose can maneuver its seven to ten pounds out of the air with the skill of the finest pilot.

The best time to photograph flying geese at Horicon is when the sun is very low. As the birds pass, their undersides are illuminated for a better picture.

Horicon Refuge in Wisconsin is a perfect place for Canada geese. The Holstein cow and the Canada goose have the same food requirements—corn and alfalfa.

Just outside the Federal Refuge Headquarters building, Canada geese scoured the fields planted just for them.

The reason few live to be thirty is that life is hard for a large bird traveling with hundreds of thousands of other large birds. In addition to the problem of finding the staggering amounts of food required for so many seven- to ten-pound birds (each goose eats a half pound of food a day), there are predators, disease and the annual harvest by hunters.

But all the needs to sustain 200,000 Canada geese are met at Horicon. The food and habitat are ideal for this kind of invasion each fall and to a lesser extent in the spring.

"We could not have planned a better location for a Canada goose refuge than America's dairyland," commented Personius. "The Holstein cow and the Canada goose have the same food requirements—corn and alfalfa."

There is much of both in the Horicon Refuge. Nevertheless, the local farmers have their troubles with the geese. In spite of the 1,000-plus acres of corn, wheat and grass planted specially for the geese, it is impossible to confine the birds to the refuge. They use it as a sanctuary for roosting, watering and some feeding, but they must also feed on private lands to survive in these numbers. Therefore, Wisconsin wildlife authorities reimburse farmers for crop damage caused by hordes of hungry birds that invade their fields. In 1974, the worst year on record, $24,725 was paid for crop damage, according to State Refuge Manager Jim Bell, to sixty-two Horicon Zone farmers. The Wisconsin Department of Natural Resources owns and manages an additional 10,000 acres south of the federal refuge.

Crop damage is a relatively new problem at Horicon, because the geese have only recently arrived there in great numbers. In fact, before 1942 there were no geese at all at Horicon.

It all started in 1940, when the State of Wisconsin began buying land in the southern third of the marsh to create a duck refuge, specifically redhead nesting habitat. The following year, the U.S. Fish and Wildlife Service started acquiring the northern two-thirds of the huge marshland for the same purpose. With each passing year, more and more geese have made Horicon their stopover between Canadian nesting grounds on Hudson Bay and their final wintering areas in southern Illinois and nearby Missouri, Kentucky and Tennessee. Their numbers have increased from 2,000 in 1948 to 51,000 in 1958 to 210,000

In spite of the thousands of acres of grain planted for the geese in the refuge, they made daily forage trips to the surrounding farmland. Crop-damage losses have increased as the flock has grown.

in 1972. The number of birds has leveled off since 1972, but they now spend about three months in the Horicon area instead of just a few weeks.

Large concentrations of Canada geese have made it possible for sportsmen to participate in a carefully managed hunt in areas surrounding the refuge. Each hunter is allowed to take one goose, but first he must be selected to receive a hunting permit as a successful applicant in a lottery. In 1975, 28,000 permits were issued and over 20,000 geese were harvested.

The increasing number of geese spending a rather lengthy

period of time in Wisconsin has caused some problems for Mississippi Flyway game managers. This so-called "short-stopping" in Wisconsin of 75 percent of the Mississippi Flyway flock has seriously limited goose-hunting opportunities in the states south of Wisconsin. For that reason, the Fish and Wildlife Service experimented in 1966 with a hazing program that was intended to move the geese south earlier than they were ready to go. Reporting on the experiment for *National Wildlife* magazine, I witnessed a complete fiasco. The only effect the hazing airplanes and helicopters had on the geese was to move them out of the refuge and onto private land, creating even greater crop damage. The program was abandoned. (As this book was being printed, the U.S. Fish and Wildlife Service was again hazing the geese in an attempt to move 100,000 of them south soon after they arrived in the Horicon area.)

The aborted hazing program only proved what was already well known: that the geese were not ready to continue south in 1966 and nothing could move them.

The hazing effort did attract considerable national attention. At the height of the big push to move the geese south, both the NBC (Huntley–Brinkley) and the CBS (Walter Cronkite) news departments sent teams of photographers and reporters to this obscure spot in rural Wisconsin to report on the program.

Local TV stations still cover the goose phenomenon at Horicon, but now more as an indicator of the change of seasons.

Though fall is the well-known time to see geese at Horicon, they do pass through the area on their way north in the spring. The breeding instinct is so strong in the spring, however, that they stop for only a few weeks before hurrying on to the Canadian nesting grounds. But spring is an excellent time to see other kinds of waterfowl and songbirds at Horicon. Kit and I have enjoyed many spring days walking the dikes and checking new arrivals. We have been particularly interested in the yellow-headed blackbirds that nest there. Over the years, we have seen about 125 species at the marsh through all seasons. If you want to make your own count, an official bird list and maps of the refuge are available at federal headquarters.

Getting excited about the birds at Horicon is not new. Humans have been going there for centuries to see birds. When

Fish and Wildlife Service biologists count the geese at Horicon from an airplane once a week during the peak period.

the Winnebago Indians controlled the Rock River Waterway which drains Horicon, they called it the "Winnebago Marsh."

Satterlee Clark visited Horicon in 1830 and found Chief White Breast at the head of 2,000 Winnebagos. They knew Horicon Marsh as a paradise for hunting of wildfowl.

C. A. Hart, in 1885, states:

> Nearly every species of migratory water-fowl known to the inland waters of North America can be found here. Specimens of over 20 varieties of wild ducks are known to have been taken during the season in 1883. Wood-ducks, widgeon, spoon-bill and red head are plentiful. The canvas-back is occasionally taken, and when the autumn flight southward fairly sets in, the pin-tails seem to outnumber all other varieties.

And so man has long looked to Horicon as a place to find respite from the problems of everyday life. Even today in our hustle-bustle world, the sight and sound of ducks and geese evoke in us a feeling of contentment. A feeling that all is right with the world.

VISITOR TIPS

Recommended time to visit: First two weeks in October is usually when the masses of geese reach their peak, but spectacular numbers can be seen from mid-September through November.

Clothing: October in Wisconsin is usually sunny and clear, but unpredictable—fluctuating between warm Indian summer and crisp fall weather. So typical autumn clothing is in order here—jackets and sweaters. There are as yet no foot trails, so hiking boots are not necessary for your Horicon visit.

Lodging: Motels are located in Waupun, Horicon, Mayville and Beaver Dam.

Restaurants: Waupun, Horicon and Mayville have restaurants. There is also one along Route 49, the Wild Goose Inn, which has the advantage of offering dinners with a panoramic view of the Horicon Marsh and its geese.

Camping: A private campground in the town of Horicon offers every facility a camper could want.

Picnic Areas: There are no picnic facilities in the refuge, but there is a small picnic area just west of the refuge on Highway 49 where we have eaten lunch while large flocks of geese passed directly overhead.

Reservations: Advance reservations are probably not necessary. For motel and camping information, write:

> Refuge Manager
> Horicon National Wildlife Refuge
> Route 2
> Mayville, Wisconsin 53050

Rest Rooms: There is a Fish and Wildlife Service Rest Stop with toilets on Highway 49.

Telephone: In any of the nearby towns.

Gasoline: All of the communities near the marsh have gasoline.

Groceries: In addition to grocery stores in all of the surrounding towns, there are cheese factories in Mayville with outlet stores open to the public.

Hospital: Waupun.

Airport: The closest airport serving commercial flights is Mitchell Field in Milwaukee (about 75 miles south of Horicon).

Bird List: Birders can pick up a checklist of 198 species at the Federal Headquarters building just off Highway Z.

12

Tule-Klamath-Malheur:
Sound of a Million Wings

These northwestern lakes, hemmed in on all sides by mountains and forests and deserts, are a bottleneck where birds must *stop on their way south. They are at their best in October, when the vast numbers of birds almost blot out the sun. They also are no mean producers of young birds; here thousands of young chicks first see the light of day.*

—Roger Tory Peterson

The accounts of our early explorers telling of the abundance of game have always fascinated me. I have tried to visualize the sights Lewis and Clark and others had of buffalo and elk "as far as the eye could see." The thought of "wild fowl" blackening the sky has been mind-boggling. Was there really that much wildlife?

Yes, there was. In fact, there is at least one place in America where the wildfowl still blacken the sky. The place is Tule Lake National Wildlife Refuge, one of five units in the Klamath Basin National Wildlife Refuges, on the California–Oregon border. Tule Lake and Lower Klamath are the two units Roger Peterson listed as birding hot spots. Strategically located on the Pacific Flyway, Tule and Klamath are stopping places for most

Pintails filled the sky, just as they must have when the early explorers first arrived in the Tule-Klamath area of northern California.

of the ducks and geese flying south to central California, Mexico and South America from northern Canada, Alaska and Siberia. These fresh-water lakes are oases along the Pacific Flyway where waterfowl find the necessary food, cover and water needed to support their semiannual flights north and south. This was the incentive that brought me to northern California.

For the only time during the fieldwork for this book, Kit stayed at home. We figured it would take six days of very hard driving from Wisconsin to northern California and home again, so I decided to fly alone.

At Klamath Falls, Oregon, on October 1, I rented a car and drove to the Klamath Basin Wildlife Refuges headquarters, 5

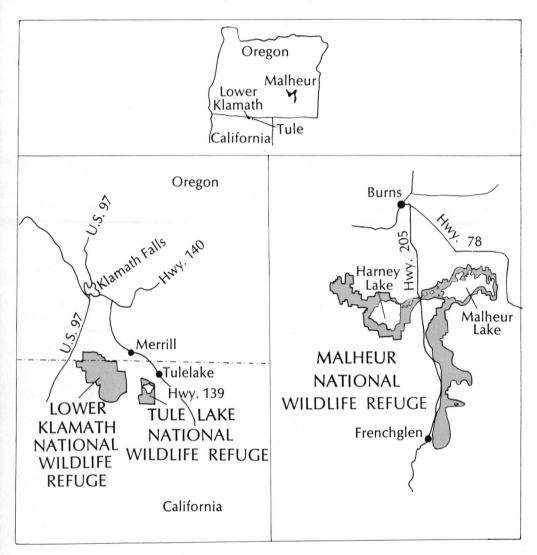

miles west of the little town of Tulelake, California. Following a short orientation by Refuge Manager Robert Fields and Biologist Ed O'Neill, I was given a map and bird list and directed to the start of the 15-mile auto tour road around Tule Lake.

Tule is a large, shallow diked lake bordered on the west by high cliffs called Sheepy Ridge and on the other three sides by

I heard white-crowned sparrows everywhere at Tule Lake, and mixed with them I found my first golden-crowned sparrows.

rich farmland planted in grain and potatoes. As I drove beneath the cliffs, I started what turned out to be my best list of songbirds for the week. I found white-crowned sparrows, feeding in the sage, rabbit brush and juniper, to be the most abundant songbirds in the area, followed by Brewer's blackbirds and then by a new bird for me, the golden-crowned sparrow. Golden-

Everywhere I looked—on the water, in the sky, against the far mountains—I saw ducks. Two million waterfowl stop at Tule and Lower Klamath each October as they work their way down the Pacific Flyway.

crowns look much like white-crowned sparrows, but wear a deep-yellow cap. Both "crowned" sparrows, like their white-throated cousin, sing lively and cheerful songs even in the fall. As I drove along, California quail were everywhere—on the gravel road, in the trees and on the boulders at the base of the cliff. In less than a mile south of headquarters I had my first view of Tule Lake waterfowl. On the water, bobbing like a million apples in the world's largest barrel, were more ducks than I had known existed. From the cattails just outside the car all the way to infinity were ducks!

Pintails; mallards; northern shovelers; cinnamon and green-winged teal; pied-billed, western and eared grebes; ruddy ducks; canvasbacks and redheads; American widgeon (baldpates); gadwalls and American coots were there in great numbers.

During the previous year's peaks, estimates showed that the refuge held 605,000 pintails, 90,000 mallards, 109,000 American widgeon (baldpates), 19,000 gadwalls, 85,000 northern shovelers, 32,000 ruddy ducks, 9,000 teal and 31,000 canvasbacks. Add these to huge numbers of geese and you get an idea of the remarkable population of birds massed there.

Ed O'Neill told me that the waterfowl numbers peak in late October, when nearly 2 million ducks and geese are present.

The reason I was here in early October was that I was likely to see more species of birds then than later in the month. It was still early enough for me to catch the first migrants as well as to see all the species that would be there in greater numbers in another few weeks. It was estimated that there were over a half million waterfowl on Tule during the period I was there. Another reason for arriving in early October was that the birding is better before the waterfowl hunting season opens on the second weekend of the month.

Working my way around the south end of Tule, I started up the east side, where I had my first view of Mount Shasta, a 14,000-foot snow-covered peak looming over the lake. That magnificent mountain was a perfect backdrop for some kind of wildlife photograph! As I headed directly north on the east side, where the road crosses the railroad at the grain elevator, I noticed large flocks of white-fronted geese sideslipping out of the

A little patience paid off as flocks of white-fronted geese landed right in front of me along the loop road through Lower Klamath Wildlife Refuge.

sky and landing in the marsh to the left of the road . . . a perfect situation for the wildlife scenic I wanted. I quickly set up my camera with a 400mm lens on the tripod and waited for the next flock to arrive. Moments later about 20 geese flew in, and I pushed the button just as they crossed the snowy face of Mount Shasta.

After I reshot this photo several times, a thrilling thing happened. The whitefronts were suddenly frightened and took off en masse. At least 5,000 geese rose in one great flock and passed across Mount Shasta. I shot as many photos as I could while the big birds moved through the scene. When it was over, I was tense with excitement and eager to see the processed photographs.

The geese I caught on film were but a fraction of the 200,000 whitefronts that stop at Tule and Klamath each fall. They leave the refuges in April and May and fly to northern Canada and Alaska, where within a matter of days they will have built nests and laid their eggs. Bad weather often destroys nests, and when it does, a poor hatch of youngsters results. The same birds are back in Tule-Klamath by September with the young of the year that have survived the nesting season.

The same general story is true for the 250,000 snow and Ross's geese that stop at Tule-Klamath. Some of them fly all the way to Wrangel Island, off the Siberian coast. Bad weather conditions during the last three nesting seasons before I was there had seriously reduced white goose populations. Only a few of the birds had arrived back by early October, but reports from the north were encouraging.

Among the first snow geese to arrive were two that had teamed up with a crippled Ross's goose. A Ross's looks like a miniature snow goose. The three were across the dike from me as I edged the car to the side of the road for a photograph. The Ross's is decidedly smaller and has a shorter neck. It was fortunate that I should see my first Ross's standing with two snows for comparison.

My biggest thrill, however, was yet to come. Driving up on the east side of Tule, I came to the bridge over Lost River, the main source of water for Tule Lake. As I approached I could see large masses of ducks sitting on the river, but it was not until I drove down the gravel road paralleling the river that I realized just how many ducks were there.

I stepped out of the car with my camera at the ready. Before me lay the largest flock of mallards and pintails I could imagine. Floating only inches apart, they spread from shore to shore on the Lost River! After I had shot several photographs of the profu-

I was lucky to get this rare shot of a Ross's goose (left) with two snow geese for size comparison. Seeing them together made it easy to identify the Ross's.

It was wall-to-wall ducks for a quarter-mile stretch along the Lost River where it empties into Tule Lake.

Chatterbox of the swamp, this long-billed marsh wren scolded me as I tried to get closer to a flock of sitting ducks on the Lost River.

sion of floating ducks, they suddenly flushed. All those wings beating against water and air sounded like the roar of a freight train. The throng of squawking, flapping birds rose above the water, circled once in perfect light, then turned and flew between the sun and me . . . and the sky darkened! I don't know exactly how many ducks were in this single flock, but there were at least 10,000. I don't expect ever to see more ducks in one flock, and I consider that moment one of the highlights of my birding career. I became a believer in the descriptions our early explorers gave of great flocks of wildfowl.

Most of the second day of my trip was spent in Lower Klamath, only 11 miles west of Tule. Klamath is made up of several bodies of water and marshland separated by dikes and farmed land. One of the nice features of California Highway 161 (State Line Road) is that it traverses the northern sector of Lower Klamath. This permits people passing by to enjoy the waterfowl. There are two parking areas called "Wildlife View Points" along Route 161. I am an advocate of bringing wildlife and people together at our National Wildlife Refuges. Exposure like that on Route 161 will ultimately benefit the Fish and Wildlife Service program.

For those who stop along 161, birding is excellent. In addition to the common ducks and geese found earlier in Tule, I spotted American avocets (lighter than at Bear River now that they had fall plumage), a flock of water (American) pipits, ring-billed gulls, long-billed dowitchers and white pelicans.

Turning at the well-marked entrance, I was presented with a choice: "Long Tour Route, 15.5 miles—suggested travel time 2 hours," or "Short Tour Route, 6.5 miles—suggested time 1 hour." I took the Long Tour Route, but would drive both roads before the day was over.

The roads through Klamath, like those at Tule, are gravel. There had been no rain for six weeks or more, and all roads were extremely dusty. A cloud of dust followed my car, and quick stops meant that I was immediately engulfed. This was not good for my cameras.

Even so, it was worth putting up with the dust to see the birds. In fact, some species were right in the middle of the dusty roads. Ring-necked pheasants, for example, seemed to

Members of the Central Oregon Audubon Society counted water birds along Highway 161 (State Line Road) at Lower Klamath National Wildlife Refuge in early October.

love to peck around in the gravel in search of spilled grain from sharecroppers' trucks. At one point in Klamath, I counted 25 pheasants in a 30-yard stretch ahead of me. Barn and cliff swallows, savannah sparrows and blackbirds also frequented the gravel.

In my search for tricolored blackbirds known to inhabit the

Ed O'Neill bagging a pintail.

Biologist Ed O'Neill was trapping and banding ducks for a research project at Lower Klamath National Wildlife Refuge. He allowed me to photograph part of his catch before he released them. All three of these species—mallard, pintail and redhead—are common migrants at Tule-Klamath.

Mallard.

area, I found myself checking hundreds of red-winged black-birds, but I never did spot a redwing with white instead of yellow on its chevron. At one place in Klamath where a little steel bridge crosses a ditch, blackbirds were lined up on the railings. I stopped to check for tricolored and found 5 different species in this flock of about 20 birds on my "blackbird bridge." There were several yellow-headed, Brewer's and red-winged blackbirds, cowbirds and one starling. No tricolored.

At another point, which must have been about as far from the main highway (161) as I could get, I found a flock of several whistling swans sitting among the geese and ducks. This group was a vanguard of 3,000 to 4,000 whistlers that would be in Tule-Klamath before the end of October. During spring migrations, up to 10,000 whistlers visit the lakes.

Later in the day, I met Ed O'Neill on his way to band ducks. I followed him as he unlocked a gate and went down an obscure dike road to large chicken-wire duck traps. The barley used as bait had gathered a catch of about 15 birds, consisting of mallards, pintails, redheads and one American coot. Ed was banding only mallards and pintails, so after I made a few photos, he released all but the 2 species to be banded. Then I watched as Ed's experienced hands carefully placed a num-bered aluminum ring on each duck's leg. A delicate squeeze with pliers tightened the band, and the bird was released. As the ducks flew out over the water one at a time, I wondered if and where those bands would be recovered. Through years of banding birds, we have learned a great deal about many species.

I asked Ed how all those ducks and geese found enough food at Tule-Klamath. He told me that the areas in the refuge were farmed by sharecroppers under an agreement to leave about 30 percent of the crop standing. In addition, Ed said, large acreages are farmed just for the birds, such as the 2,000 acres around the water's edge of Tule planted in barley, oats, wheat, bluegrass, fescue and alfalfa. All this grain, plus the waste grain from thousands of acres throughout the basin, plus the natural aquatic plant and animal life in the lakes provided more than enough.

Both Tule Lake and Lower Klamath were, at one time,

Mule deer were plentiful at Tule Lake. They usually just watched from the ditches as I drove past. Stopping the car for photographs didn't seem to disturb them.

much larger bodies of water until they were dried up by the Federal Government to reclaim land for agriculture in the early 1900s. In 1850, when the first settlers arrived in northern California, Tule Lake encompassed some 150 square miles.

In 1905, California and Oregon entered into an agreement with the Federal Government which said the government could have all the land reclaimed from under the existing lakes. Water diversion began first at Tule, where all but 13,000 acres was dried up. This fertile land was then periodically opened for homesteading and was quickly converted to agriculture. Lower Klamath marshes actually dried up and were a dust bowl for twenty years.

In 1908, a farsighted Teddy Roosevelt ordered the creation of the world's first refuge for waterfowl from 81,619 acres of Lower Klamath, later reduced to 47,583 acres. In 1928, 11,000 acres in and around Tule Lake were set aside as a refuge, then enlarged to 34,988 acres. However, it was not until 1964, when the Kuchel Act was passed, that both of these vital areas were finally removed from the pressures of homesteading.

Roosevelt and others were farsighted enough to put these wildlife areas under the direction of the Fish and Wildlife Service (at that time called the Bureau of Biological Survey), for their existence is essential to the health of the entire Pacific Flyway, consisting today of 10 million or more ducks and geese, and far greater numbers of marsh, water and shore birds.

I also asked Ed about the occurrence of botulism, which plagues most western waterfowl areas. He said that they have had several good years, with only a couple of thousand birds succumbing to the bacteria. During bad years, many thousands die of the strange malady.

By the end of the second day at Tule-Klamath, I knew that these areas were not going to produce a big bird list. I had seen only 63 species at that time. If Kit had been along, we would have listed more.

On my third and last day in the Lower Klamath Basin, Refuge Manager Bob Fields spent much of his Saturday showing me areas I had missed. Bob started the day by welcoming fifteen members of the Central Oregon Audubon Society who had driven from Bend, Oregon, to spend the weekend. After the Auduboners left on their trip through Klamath, we returned to Tule for more scenics of geese against Mount Shasta. While photographing, I noticed mallards flushing from the ditch behind me, but didn't pay much attention to them until I heard a rush of air as if someone had turned on a big fan. I wheeled around in time to see a golden eagle power-dive into the middle of the mallard flock. It had intended to knock a duck out of the

Sneaking over a little rise, Refuge Manager Bob Fields and I got close to an island of white pelicans at the southeast corner of Tule Lake.

In the cliffs surrounding Tule, we found a variety of hawks and owls. This ferruginous hawk played the thermals with a marsh hawk, a prairie falcon and a golden eagle.

air, but had missed. It all happened so quickly, I didn't think to try to photograph the brown bomber.

My three days at Tule and Klamath were over. The following morning I headed north to Malheur, the third of the big three refuges in the southern Oregon/northern California area. Malheur is about 32 miles south of Burns, Oregon, some 280 miles east and north of Tule and Klamath.

MALHEUR

Malheur is surprisingly different in appearance from Tule and Klamath. It is drier, and there is more character to the landscape. Its 181,000 acres consist of broad shallow marshes, small ponds, irrigated meadows, alkaline lakes and grass and sagebrush uplands, all surrounded by high buttes which give the area a Western-movie flavor.

I had been in Malheur only a few hours when I began to suspect that there were management problems. The excessive number of cattle grazing in the refuge was a grim reminder of my visit a few months earlier to Bharatpur Bird Sanctuary in India—one of the greatest in the world, but now being destroyed by cattle. The text of the self-guided auto tour explained that cattle in Malheur are being used as a management tool to keep grass down, but when I questioned refuge personnel the following day, my suspicions were confirmed. Long-term grazing rights have created problems with no immediate solution short of a big political fight, which the Fish and Wildlife Service has avoided. It seemed obvious to me that Malheur and its wildlife would benefit greatly from a reduction in the number of cattle on the refuge, if not total removal of the cattle.

October 5, when I arrived, was a Sunday, so there was no one in the headquarters office with whom to talk. I picked up literature at its fine natural history museum and started off on the Blitzen Valley self-guided auto tour, a 42-mile one-way drive ending in Frenchglen at the southernmost tip of the refuge.

The weather was cool and sunny, and I was happy to be back in a working area after my long drive from Tule. The guide sheet and the twenty-nine numbered stations along the route were very well prepared. This three-to-five-hour drive is a credit to the refuge. The auto tour alone may account for the fact that annual visitations were increasing at the rate of 23 percent a year.

In the Blitzen Valley, however, I was disappointed to find very little birdlife along the route. Though I recorded 7 new species for this chapter, I expected more. Not only were the species lacking, but the numbers of ducks and geese were insignificant compared with those at Tule-Klamath. I learned the following day during my talks with refuge personnel that Malheur is far better as a birding spot in spring when the Blitzen Valley is flooded with snow waters flowing off Steens Mountain. I also discovered that fall numbers of waterfowl are down from those recorded five and ten years ago.

At Station Number 7, the tour-guide text tells about a tower built by the CCC in 1939 to serve as a fire lookout. Golden eagles have tried to nest on it in recent years. I saw no nest on the tower, but across the road and above the butte, two golden eagles soared on thermals rising from the hot sage-covered plains. The huge, dark brown birds hung motionless at the edge of the butte.

The tour-guide text was surprisingly accurate again at Station Number 13 where it said greater sandhill cranes would be using the rehabilitated grainfields as a staging area before migrating south to the Central Valley of California. Sure enough, the field contained 50 or more greater sandhills feeding and preening in the golden stubble. As I watched, several more families of sandies joined the flocks. Their mournful trumpets reminded me of our days on the big lesser sandhill staging area of the Platte River in Nebraska the previous March.

Just before turning into the Buena Vista area beyond Station Number 14, I had my biggest thrill at Malheur. Six great birds, 2 of them snow-white, flew over the car and landed in the pond to the west. Fumbling for my binoculars and trying to stop the car at the same time, I looked wide-eyed at 6 trumpeter swans—4 cygnets and their parents. A quick check of my Peterson *Field Guide* showed me the difference between whistlers and trumpeters. Adult trumpeters lack the bright yellow spot

The Blitzen Valley Auto Tour is well prepared and well marked. This 42-mile one-way drive took me through a sampling of Malheur's shallow marshland, small ponds and irrigated meadows.

that the whistlers have at the top of the bill. The trumpeter cygnets are a much darker gray, and their bills are pink, tipped by black.

Management of the trumpeter swan is one of the great success stories of the endangered-species program. Twenty-five years ago, the trumpeter was on the verge of extinction. Careful management and strict protection brought our largest swan back.

The last time I had seen a trumpeter was in 1956 at the National Elk Refuge in Jackson, Wyoming. The pair breeding there had been among the few remaining birds in existence. Now trumpeter swans are found in many areas of the West.

Five female common mergansers swam out from under a little bridge I drove over on the Blitzen Valley Auto Tour at Malheur.

As the Blitzen Valley Tour text predicted, I found a golden eagle riding the thermals at Station Number 7. The tour text was surprisingly accurate, which may account for Malheur's 50,000 visitations each year.

Driving north on Route 205 through Malheur National Wildlife Refuge, I spotted a large flock of greater sandhill cranes dancing and feeding only 100 yards off the highway.

These two women driving the Blitzen Valley auto tour didn't see the great horned owl until it was too late.

Near the end of the auto tour, at Station Number 29, I read in the text about the history of P Ranch, a legendary cattle empire of the late 1800s. I had been told that the tower at P Ranch was a perching spot for turkey vultures. These buzzards sit on the metal fire tower at any time of the day or night. It had begun to rain by the time I reached P Ranch, but there were still 2 turkey vultures on the tower. I found 20 more in the protection of the huge cottonwood trees along the road.

Just beyond P Ranch is Page Spring Campground, where I spent the night. It is a primitive campground with only picnic tables and outhouses. This campground and the Malheur Environmental Field Station, over 40 miles away near headquarters, are the only lodging facilities except the hotel at the little crossroads of Frenchglen, 4 miles west of Page Spring.

Gasoline can be a problem in the Malheur area, and I kept a watchful eye on the gauge. The gas station at Frenchglen is the only one outside of Burns, 60 miles to the north.

Just before dark at the campground, I heard a sweet thrush-like song and spotted a Townsend's solitaire, an unimpressive gray bird that looks somewhat like a mockingbird.

The following day, October 6, was one of the few rainy days that country had seen in months. The rain made refuge roads impassable and forced me to take the hardtop road (Route 205) back to headquarters. En route I found another grainfield with greater sandhill cranes feeding. They were not as "spooky" as I expected, and I was able to photograph them from the road as they fed and danced. I presumed their dancing was recreation and exercise in preparation for their flight to central California.

My inquiry at refuge headquarters revealed that in the fall the best places to see waterfowl and shore birds were Malheur Lake and Stinking Lake, to the north. However, Malheur Lake was physically inaccessible while I was there, and Stinking Lake was no longer open to the public at any time.

I suggested to refuge personnel that they should improve public access to Malheur Lake so that visiting bird watchers could see the best at Malheur during peak spring and fall migrations.

I do not recommend traveling a great distance to see Malheur in the fall. Spring is undoubtedly a better time for listing all kinds of birds, particularly when the Blitzen Valley is flooded and the tules do not mask the ponds.

In either season, the best place to see songbirds is at refuge headquarters, P Ranch and Wetzel Patrol Station. Waterfowl hot spots open to the public include Buena Vista Station, Cole Island Dike (if you can get in), Krumbo Pond and Benson Pond.

My trip to Tule-Klamath-Malheur produced a bird list of 85 species (some of them life listers), and I saw great masses of ducks probably unmatched anywhere. If you want to experience the thrills our early explorers had in viewing unbelievable numbers of "wild fowl," Tule and Klamath in October is the place to be.

VISITOR TIPS

Recommended time to visit: Tule-Klamath—late September to freezing. Malheur—mid-March through early April.

Clothing: Fall clothing, including a warm jacket for early mornings and late afternoons. Also, comfortable walking shoes are recommended.

Lodging: For Tule and Klamath, motels are located in Klamath Falls, Tulelake and Merrill. In the Malheur area, Burns, Oregon, has motels. Or, you may be able to make arrangements to stay at the Malheur Environmental Field Station, which has dormitory and semiprivate rooms.

Restaurants: Tulelake, Klamath Falls and Merrill have restaurants. If you are at Malheur, Burns has restaurants, or, if you have a reservation, you may be able to eat at the Field Station mess hall.

Camping: For Tule and Klamath, campgrounds are located at Lava Bed National Monument, Tulelake, Klamath Falls and Merrill. At Malheur, the Field Station has trailer hookups for campers. Page Spring Campground, near Frenchglen, is 40 miles up the Blitzen Valley from Malheur headquarters and offers only primitive camping.

Picnic Areas: Lava Bed National Monument, near Tule-Klamath, and Page Spring Campground, at Malheur, have picnic tables.

Reservations: Write ahead for motel and camping information to:

> Tule-Klamath:
> Refuge Manager
> Klamath Basin National Wildlife Refuge
> Route 1, Box 74
> Tule Lake, California 96134
> (916) 667-2231

> Malheur:
> Refuge Manager
> Malheur National Wildlife Refuge
> P.O. Box 113
> Burns, Oregon 97720

> For reservations at the Malheur Field Station:
> Malheur Environmental Field Station
> P.O. Box 989
> Burns, Oregon 97720

Rest Rooms: They are located at refuge headquarters, at Lava Bed National Monument and on Lower Klamath in the Tule-Klamath area. At Malheur, rest rooms are provided in the museum at headquarters and at Page Spring, Buena Vista Station and Krumbo Reservoir.

Telephone: Public phones may be found in Tulelake, Merrill and Klamath Falls at the Klamath Basin Refuges. At Malheur there is one at Frenchglen and another at the Malheur Environmental Field Station. There is also one along Highway 161 near the Malheur headquarters turnoff.

Gasoline: Tulelake, Klamath Falls and Merrill offer gasoline in the Tule-Klamath region. Burns and Frenchglen are the closest if you are at Malheur. Keep an eye on your gas gauge.

Groceries: Tulelake, Klamath Falls and Merrill have grocery stores in the Klamath Basin area. For Malheur, you can do your shopping in Frenchglen and in Burns.

Hospital: Klamath Falls has a hospital. If you're at Malheur, Burns, Oregon, 32 miles from headquarters, has a hospital.

Airport: For Tule and Klamath, Klamath Falls is the closest airport. For Malheur, Boise, Idaho, is the closest.

Bird List: A list of 249 birds is available at Klamath Basin Refuge Headquarters for Tule and Klamath. At Malheur, you can pick one up at the natural history museum at refuge headquarters. The Malheur list includes 230 species.

Organizations of Interest to Birders

National Audubon Society
950 Third Avenue
New York, New York 10022

PUBLICATIONS
Audubon magazine
American Birds

National Wildlife Federation
1412 Sixteenth Street, N.W.
Washington, D.C. 20036

PUBLICATIONS
National Wildlife magazine
International Wildlife magazine
Ranger Rick's Nature Magazine

American Birding Association
P.O. Box 6
Dunlap, Tennessee 37327

PUBLICATION
Birding

Cornell Laboratory of Ornithology
159 Sapsucker Woods Road
Ithaca, New York 14850

PUBLICATIONS
The Living Bird
Members' Newsletter

American Ornithologists Union, Inc.
National Museum of Natural History
Smithsonian Institution
Washington, D.C. 20560

PUBLICATION
The Auk

Brooks Bird Club
707 Warwood Avenue
Wheeling, West Virginia 26003

PUBLICATIONS
The Redstart
The Mailbag

Cooper Ornithological Society
c/o Harold F. Mayfield
9235 River Road
Waterville, Ohio 43566

PUBLICATIONS
The Condor
Pacific Coast Avifauna

Hawk Mountain Sanctuary Association
R.D. 2
Kempton, Pennsylvania 19529

PUBLICATION
Members' Newsletter

Wilson Ornithological Society
c/o Jerome A. Jackson
Department of Zoology
Mississippi State University
Mississippi State, Mississippi 39762

PUBLICATION
The Wilson Bulletin

Bibliography

Bond, James. *Native Birds of Mount Desert Island*. Philadelphia: Academy of Natural Science, 1971.

Brett, James J., and Nagy, Alexander C. *Feathers in the Wind*. Kempton, Pennsylvania: Hawk Mountain Sanctuary Association, 1973.

Canadian Wildlife Service. *Sea-birds of Bonaventure Island*. Ottawa: Information Canada, 1973.

Harrison, Hal H. *A Field Guide to Birds' Nests*. Boston: Houghton Mifflin, 1975.

Harwood, Michael. *The View from Hawk Mountain*. New York: Charles Scribner's Sons, 1973.

Heintzelman, Donald S. *Autumn Hawk Flights*. New Brunswick, New Jersey: Rutgers University Press, 1975.

Lane, James A. *A Birder's Guide to the Rio Grande Valley of Texas*. Denver: L & P Photography, 1971.

Lane, James. A. *A Birder's Guide to Southeastern Arizona*. Denver: L & P Photography, 1974.

Lane, James A., and Tveten, John L. *A Birder's Guide to the Texas Coast*. Denver: L & P Photography, 1974.

Mélancon, Claude. *Percé and Bonaventure Island's Seabirds*. Montreal: Editions Du Jour, 1974

Peterson, Roger Tory. *Birds Over America*. New York: Dodd, Mead & Company, 1948.

Peterson, Roger Tory. *A Field Guide to the Birds*. Boston: Houghton Mifflin, 1947.

Peterson, Roger Tory. *A Field Guide to Birds of Texas*. Boston: Houghton Mifflin, 1963.

Peterson, Roger Tory. *A Field Guide to Western Birds*. Boston: Houghton Mifflin, 1969.

Peterson, Roger Tory, and Chalif, Edward L. *A Field Guide to Mexican Birds*. Boston: Houghton Mifflin, 1973.

Peterson, Roger Tory, and Fisher, James. *Wild America*. Boston: Houghton Mifflin, 1955.

Pettingill, Olin Sewall, Jr. *The Bird Watcher's America*. New York: McGraw-Hill, 1965.

Robbins, Chandler S.; Brunn, Bertel, and Zim, Herbert S. *Birds of North America*. New York: Golden Press, 1966.

Robertson, William B., Jr. *Everglades—The Park Story*. Coral Gables, Florida: University of Miami Press, 1959.

Stirrett, George M. *The Spring Birds of Point Pelee National Park*. Ottawa: Information Canada, 1973.

Stone, Witmer. *Bird Studies at Old Cape May*, Volumes I and II. New York: Dover Publications, 1965.

Zim, Herbert S. *A Guide to Everglades National Park and Nearby Florida Keys*. New York: Golden Press, 1960.

Page Guide to the Birds

NOTE: *Many common birds not listed here were seen and recorded, but are not mentioned in the text. The bird species recorded during our birding year totaled 402.*